DATA STRUCTURES AND ADVANCED ALGORITHMS

Rachel Xin, Tony Lee, and Elisabeth Feng

ABOUT THE AUTHORS

Rachel Xin

Rachel Xin is a senior at Troy High School, where she participates in the Troy Tech magnet program in the Computer Science and Cyber Security Pathway. She is a member of the National Honor Society and has received the Fullerton Rotary Top 100 Award, Principal's Honor Roll Award, Scholar Athlete Award, and National AP Scholar Award for her academic achievements. She also specializes in Cisco in her cybersecurity team, placing Top 20 nationally in the CyberPatriot competition Platinum Open Division. Rachel is also the President of Heart of Hope, a nonprofit organization founded on providing special needs children with fun, learning opportunities including music, sports, and crafts. Additionally, she is the Fundraising Chair for STEMup4Youth, an organization dedicated toward inspiring underserved children to pursue science through STEM-related activities. She is also the leader of Heart of Music, where she performs at local senior centers. Her extensive volunteer experience has earned her the President's Volunteer Gold Service Award twice. At school, she has been on the Varsity Tennis Team since freshman year as a doubles player. She also has experience in Artificial Intelligence, after successfully completing the Stanford Pre-Collegiate AI for Robots Course. In her free time, she enjoys drawing and listening to music.

Tony Lee

Tony Lee is a technical leader and product manager at The Boeing Company, where he has been recognized for his excellence as both a leader and mentor. An accomplished industry professional, he has collected a number of awards, including the IT Business Award from the Vice President of Boeing and the Pride and Achievement Award. He received his BS in Information and Computer Science (with Magna Cum Laude) from University of California, Irvine; his MS in Networked Systems from University of California, Irvine; his MS in Software Development and Management from Rochester Institute of Technology; his MBA from Capella University (with a perfect 4.0 GPA); and his MBA from Colorado Technical University. In addition, he has received several certificates in programming and agile management from various universities including Carnegie Mellon, MIT, and Stanford. He is in the Doctoral program for Big Data Analytics. Tony is a National Science Foundation Scholar and a member of the American Scholars National Honor Society. Tony has also published several articles about software engineering and the optimization of the information technology process, and he has served as a conference paper reviewer for the Association for Computing Machinery (ACM).

Elisabeth Feng

Elisabeth Feng is a senior in the Advance Science and Engineering program at Fairmont Preparatory Academy. She is a member of the National Honor Society and is an AP Scholar with Distinction. She was voted Most Valuable Cheerleader, English Student of the Year Award, AP U.S. History Student of the Year Award, the Math Department Student of the Year Award, and Safety Star of the Day Award from FRC. Elisabeth has been on the Varsity Cheer team since Freshman year and recently co-founded the Philosophy Club after being inspired from her IB Philosophy class. As Build Captain for her robotics team, the canceled competition season came after her team had completely finished this year's robot and will dedicate the next year to the graduated seniors. Last year, she volunteered as a Funds Development Intern at Colette's Children's Home, a nonprofit organization aiding homeless single women and women with children. She has a major interest in math having already taken AP Calculus BC, Differential Equations and Linear Algebra, as well as Discrete Mathematics and Number Theory. When she's not sitting in traffic, she is eating either breakfast, lunch, or dinner.

TABLE OF CONTENTS

PREFACE — 9

CHAPTER 1: OBJECT-ORIENTATED PROGRAMMING

1.1 INTRODUCTION: OBJECT-ORIENTED PROGRAMMING — 11
1.2 WHAT DEFINES AN OBJECT-ORIENTED PROGRAMMING LANGUAGE? — 11
1.3 WHY OBJECT-ORIENTED? — 11
1.4 CLASSES — 12
1.5 OBJECTS — 15
1.6 REFERENCE DATA TYPES VS. PRIMITIVE DATA TYPES — 16
1.7 INHERITANCE — 16
1.8 POLYMORPHISM — 19
1.9 ENCAPSULATION — 22

CHAPTER 2: DATA STRUCTURES

2.1 LISTS — 25
    TRAVERSING A LIST — 25
    REMOVING AN ELEMENT FROM A LIST — 26
2.2 STACK — 27
    ADDING AND REMOVING — 27
2.3 QUEUE — 30
    ADDING AND REMOVING — 31
2.4 PRIORITY QUEUE — 33
    ADDING AND REMOVING — 34

CHAPTER 3: LINKED LIST

3.1 LINKED LIST — 41
    THE NODE CLASS — 41

	THE LINKEDLIST CLASS	42
	CREATING A LINKED LIST	45
	INSERTING TO THE FRONT OF A LINKED LIST	45
	TRAVERSING A LINKED LIST	48
	INSERTING TO THE BACK OF A LINKED LIST	49
	DELETING FROM THE FRONT OF A LINKED LIST	51
	DELETING FROM THE BACK OF A LINKED LIST	52
	CIRCULAR LINKED LIST	54
3.2	DOUBLY LINKED LIST	54
	THE NODE CLASS FOR DOUBLY LINKED LIST	54
	CREATING A DOUBLY LINKED LIST	55
	INSERTING AFTER NODE N	56
	REMOVE DATA	58

CHAPTER 4: RECURSION

4.1	INTRODUCTION: RECURSION	63
4.2	RECURSION	63
4.3	WHY RECURSION?	65
4.4	WORD BREAK	69

CHAPTER 5: SORTING

5.1	INTRODUCTION: SORTING	74
5.2	SELECTION SORT	74
5.3	INSERTION SORT	79
5.4	BUBBLE SORT	84
5.5	QUICK SORT	92
5.6	MERGE SORT	111

CHAPTER 6: SEARCHING

6.1	INTRODUCTION: SEARCHING	120

6.2 BIG O NOTATION	120
6.3 LINEAR SEARCH	120
6.4 BINARY SEARCH	123
6.5 DEPTH FIRST SEARCH	128
6.6 BREADTH FIRST SEARCH	135

CHAPTER 7: ADDITIONAL TOPICS

7.1 MAX AND MIN HEAP	144
INSERTING INTO A HEAP	144
REMOVING MAX FROM A MAX HEAP	149
REMOVE ELEMENT FROM A MAX HEAP	152
7.2 DIJKSTRA'S SHORTEST PATH ALGORITHM	159
7.3 MINIMAX ALGORITHM	171
7.4 ALPHA BETA PRUNING	175
KEEP IN MIND	175
HOW IT WORKS	175

APPENDIX

1 GLOSSARY	183
2 ACKNOWLEDGEMENTS	191

Preface

WELCOME TO THE BOOK

The purpose of this book is to teach you, a budding programmer, basics of Object-Oriented Programming, data structures, and advanced algorithms using Python version 3.8. Unlike many books currently on the market, a background in math is not required to read and understand this book as the data structures and concepts will be explained in simple terms. The concepts will be broken down and thoroughly explained for any novice programmer. Python is a versatile language quickly growing in popularity and usage by programmers and companies. A bright future lies ahead for this young programming language. This book is version 3. This version encompasses all topics in previous versions covered in Python.

Chapter 1 Object-Oriented Programming

CHAPTER CONTENTS

1.1 Introduction: Object-Oriented Programming
1.2 What Defines An Object-Oriented Programming Language?
1.3 Why Object-Oriented?
1.4 Classes
1.5 Objects
1.6 Reference Data Types VS Primitive Data Types
1.7 Inheritance
1.8 Polymorphism
1.9 Encapsulation

1.1 INTRODUCTION: OBJECT-ORIENTED PROGRAMMING

Object-oriented programming (OOP) is a programming paradigm that is often overcomplicated by professionals and inexperienced computer science students alike. From the perspective of a novice programmer, colleagues and professors may seem to be speaking a secret language when they use complex terms such as "polymorphism" or "encapsulation."

In reality, the complicated terms used by professional programmers can actually be broken down into simplistic, easily-understood concepts. With some practice, anyone can understand object-oriented programming.

1.2 WHAT DEFINES AN OBJECT-ORIENTED PROGRAMMING LANGUAGE?

Simply put, object-oriented programming is a method of structuring data by placing related attributes and behaviors into individual objects. There are many OOP languages, and some of the most popular include Java, Python, and C++. This book will focus on Python to demonstrate complex topics within object-oriented programming.

All object-oriented languages have three characteristics in common: **encapsulation**, **inheritance**, and **polymorphism**. These features of object-oriented programming often blend and function concurrently. Some professionals will also argue that OOP languages all share the characteristic of **abstraction**.

Before we address these topics, we must first understand the basics of an object-oriented programming language.

1.3 WHY OBJECT-ORIENTED?

Object-oriented programming can help prevent programmers from having to "reinvent the wheel." In the same way that engineers do not have to invent a wheel today, programmers do not have to rewrite code that has already been created by someone else. With object-oriented programming, programmers can borrow code that has already been used, tested, and deemed functional without having to reinvent it.

Moreover, object-oriented programming is beneficial because of **abstraction**. Abstraction is the idea that code can be used by a programmer without knowing exactly how it works. To better understand this concept, take the example of driving a car. It is not necessary for you to know each component that comprises the brake system or understand the mechanics of the engine;

you can understand those concepts abstractly and focus on learning how to drive. Similarly, object-oriented programmers do not need to know every detail about how something works to use it in their own programs.

Finally, object-oriented programming makes delegating work easy. In OOP, the work can be divided so that different programmers contribute different **classes** that combine to make an entire functioning program, and they can do so without messing up others' work. An issue within one class will not necessarily affect another class. Relating this concept back to the example of the car, a flat tire will not directly affect the way the engine works; you just need to replace the flat tire. Similarly, if one part of a program is broken, it can be fixed without affecting other parts of the program. This aspect of object-oriented programming can make it easier for programmers to resolve errors, or **bugs**, in their code.

1.4 CLASSES

A **class** is the fundamental building block of an object-oriented language. Classes act as templates for **objects**. Think of an object as a cookie and a class as the cookie cutter. Just as the cookie cutter creates a basic design for a cookie, a class acts as a basic design for an object. To make an object, we use the class as a template to define its characteristics. Related classes can be grouped together in a single file called a module, and a collection of Python modules is called a **package**. A package, following the cookie cutter analogy, is a cabinet full of ready-for-use cookie cutters.

Let's make a new class and name it Person. To create a class, write the class keyword, followed by the name of the class and a colon. Python uses indentation to mark a block of code. Any code indented below the class definition is considered the body of the class. This is where we will later place **fields, constructors, and methods**.

FIG 1.1: *A Person class with a body*

```
1    class Person:
2        # this is the body of class "Person"
3        pass
```

In this example, the pass keyword is used as a placeholder, representing where the code will go. This keyword is used to prevent Python from throwing an error when run.

In order to add different attributes to the Person class, we will need a **constructor** to initialize, or assign values to, those fields. In Python, the properties are defined in the __init__() method, and it is called whenever an object is created. This method acts as a constructor as it initializes each new instance of the class. Parameters act as placeholders for **arguments**, or values that will be passed to constructors or methods. For the __init__() method, the first parameter will always be the self variable. Self is used to represent a specific instance of a class. Let's add some attributes to our Person class, .first_name and .last_name. In Python, it is proper naming convention to write instance variables in all lower case, with an underscore to separate specific words. Also, note that comments are written using the # sign.

FIG 1.2: A Person class with fields and a constructor

```
class Person:
    # this is the body of class "Person"

    # below is the constructor where the parameters are first_name and last_name
    def __init__(self, first_name, last_name):
        self.first_name = first_name
        self.last_name = last_name
```

In the constructor, self.first_name = first_name creates an attribute called first_name and assigns it the value in the first_name parameter. The same logic applies to the second attribute last_name.

The keyword self is also used to differentiate between instance attributes and class attributes. In the Person class, the instance attributes are the first_name and last_name. Class attributes are only used for values that are the same across every class instance, and they are located directly below the class name line. For instance, every person is of the species Homo sapiens, so let's add a class attribute called species.

FIG 1.3: *A Person class with a class attribute*

```
1    class Person:
2        # class attribute
3        species = "Homo sapiens"
4
5        # below is the constructor where the parameters are first_name and last_name
6        def __init__(self, first_name, last_name):
7            self.first_name = first_name
8            self.last_name = last_name
```

Now, let's talk about **access modifiers**, which are used to differentiate the scope of different variables. In Python, the three types of access modifiers are public, private, and protected.

Public means the variable can be accessed anywhere, both inside and out of the class. On the other hand, private variables can only be accessed inside the class, and protected variables can only be accessed in the same package.

In Python, prefixes are used to differentiate between access modifiers. For public variables, no prefix is needed. For private variables, a prefix of two underscores in front of the variable name is needed, while protected variables require a prefix of one underscore in front of the variable name.

The following example illustrates the Person class with three attributes having different access modifiers.

FIG 1.4: *A Person class with attributes having different access modifiers*

```
1    class Person:
2
3        def __init__(self, name, age, grade):
4            # public
5            self.name = name
6            # protected
7            self._age = age
8            # private
9            self.__grade = grade
```

An object of the class Person can perform certain actions, which are modeled in functions, or **methods**. Let's write a method called write_out that displays a Person object's first_name and last_name. We will be able to view the output in the **console.** The console is a simple interface that displays outputs and allows inputs from a user. Thus, we will tell the console to print the first name on a line and the last name on a separate line. As seen below, instance methods will also contain self as the first parameter.

FIG 1.5: Person class with fields, a constructor, and a method write_out

```python
class Person:
    # this is the body of class "Person"

    # below is a constructor where the parameters are
    first name and last name
    def __init__(self, first_name, last_name):
        self._first_name = first_name
        self._last_name = last_name

    # displays the object's first name and last name
    def write_out(self):
        print("First Name:", self._first_name)
        print("Last Name:", self._last_name)
```

When we **instantiate** this class and create a Person object, we have the ability to write out the first_name and last_name of the object by **invoking**, or calling into action, the method.

Now our class has a modifier, a name, protected fields, a constructor, and a method.

1.5 OBJECTS

Now that we've created a class, we can use the cookie cutter to create objects by instantiating the class and initializing its variables. Now we can create an object of class Person called person. Finally, we can invoke the method write_out to display the object's first_name and last_name.

FIG 1.6: Creating object person that invokes write_out

```python
    # this creates an object of class "Person"
    # person is a reference to that object
    # ("John", "Doe") is the argument sent to the constructor
    person = Person("John", "Doe")
    person.write_out()
```

FIG 1.7: *Result of creating an object of class Person and invoking method write_out*

```
First Name: John
Last Name: Doe
```

1.6 REFERENCE DATA TYPES VS. PRIMITIVE DATA TYPES

Variables are essential to object-oriented programming because they represent different values. Programmers manipulate variables in order to accomplish certain tasks.

It is important to note that the variable person in the above example is not the object; it merely holds a **reference** to the object. The object itself is stored in the memory of the computer.

Primitive data types are the most basic data types provided by a programming language. In Python, there are four primitive types: integers, floats, booleans, and strings. These primitive data types are basic building blocks for more sophisticated data types.

1.7 INHERITANCE

Once you create a class, you may want to create another class that shares some, but not all, of the characteristics of the original. You can do this by creating a "child" of that first class, also known as a **subclass**. Your original class then becomes the "parent," or **superclass**. When creating a subclass, the name of the superclass is written in parentheses in Python to establish the link between the subclass and the superclass. Inheritance is used when the subclass is a type of the superclass. In the example below, class Student is a subclass of class Person because Student is a type of Person, and the Student class inherits fields, constructors, and methods from its parent class.

FIG 1.8: *A parent class Person and a subclass Student*

```python
1    # this is the "parent" or superclass
2    class Person:
3        pass
4
5    # this is the "child" or subclass
6    class Student(Person):
7        pass
```

We can also create more than one subclass per parent class. In the following example, Student is a subclass of Person. Therefore, Student inherits fields, constructors, and methods from its parent class Person. Professor is also a subclass of Person, and it too inherits fields, constructors, and methods from Person. Class Person does not inherit anything from Student or Professor, and Student and Professor don't inherit anything from each other.

FIG 1.9: *A parent class Person and two subclasses Student and Professor*

```python
1    # this is the "parent" or superclass
2    class Person:
3        pass
4
5    # this is the "child" or subclass
6    class Student(Person):
7        pass
8
9    # this is also a "child" or subclass of Person
10   class Professor(Person):
11       pass
```

We can also create a subclass of a subclass. In the next example, Student is a subclass of Person again, and Sophomore is a subclass of Student. In this case, the Student class is both a subclass and a superclass. It is a subclass of Person, but a superclass of Sophomore.

FIG 1.10: *A parent class Person, a subclass Student, and a subclass of Student called Sophomore*

```python
# this is the "parent" or superclass
class Person:
    pass


# this is the "child" or subclass
class Student(Person):
    pass


# this is also a "child" or subclass of Student
class Sophomore(Student):
    pass
```

So why do we create "children," or subclasses, of classes? Well, much like children who inherit genetic characteristics from their parents, subclasses can inherit methods, fields, and constructors from their parent classes. This is the concept of **inheritance**. With inheritance, we can take advantage of code that's already been written within a parent class.

In the following example, we create an object of type Student that inherits a constructor from parent class Person. We use the keyword **super()** to access that constructor.

FIG 1.11: *A subclass Student using super() to call the constructor from parent class Person*

```python
class Student(Person):
    def __init__(self, first_name, last_name, school):
        super().__init__(first_name, last_name)
        self._school = school


student = Student("John", "Doe", "ABC School")
```

Just like how a subclass can inherit its parent's constructor, it can also inherit its parent's other methods. The inherited methods will override the subclass's methods. The importance of overriding methods will be explained in depth shortly.

FIG 1.12: A subclass Student inheriting a method from its parent class Person

```python
class Person:
    def write_out(self):
        print("I am a person.")


class Student(Person):
    # this new method overrides the method in the parent class
    def write_out(self):
        # calls method write_out from parent class
        super().write_out()


student = Student()
student.write_out()
```

FIG 1.13: Result of class Student inheriting method from parent class Person

```
I am a person.
```

1.8 POLYMORPHISM

When broken down into root words, **polymorphism** contains "poly" meaning many and "morph" meaning form. Therefore, polymorphism can be thought of as the principle of having many forms. In computer science, a class can be considered polymorphic when it has one or more methods **overridden**, or redefined, from its parent class. We can modify our code from figure 1.12 to override the method in the parent class and perform a different action when the method is called. Polymorphism helps us execute the right method at runtime. In the following example, we will create a new method inside the Student subclass that overrides the method in the parent class. Notice that the new method has the same name as the old method.

FIG 1.14: *A write_out method in subclass Student that overrides the write_out method in parent class*

```
1    class Person:
2        def write_out(self):
3            print("I am a person.")
4
5
6    class Student(Person):
7        # this new method overrides the method in the parent class
8        def write_out(self):
9            print("I am not a person.")
10
11
12   student = Student()
13   student.write_out()
```

Now, when we call the write_out method for an object of class Student, the method from the subclass, not the parent class, will execute. Therefore, we will get a different output. This is because the method from the subclass overrides the method from the parent class.

FIG 1.15: *Result of creating an object of class Student and invoking method write_out*

```
I am not a person.
```

If we create an object of the parent class Person, the method from the parent class will not be overridden by the method in the subclass Student.

FIG 1.16: Creating an object of class Person and invoking method write_out

```python
class Person:
    def write_out(self):
        print("I am a person.")



class Student(Person):
    # this new method overrides the method in the parent class
    def write_out(self):
        print("I am not a person.")



person = Person()
person.write_out()
```

FIG 1.17: Result of creating an object of class Person and invoking method write_out

```
I am a person.
```

You may be wondering how to use a parent's method after you've overridden it with a method in the subclass. This isn't impossible to do.

FIG 1.18: Calling a parent's method and overriding it

```python
class Person:
    def write_out(self):
        print("I am a person.")



class Student(Person):
    # this new method overrides the method in the parent class
    def write_out(self):
        super().write_out()
        print("Just kidding. I am not a person.")


student = Student()
student.write_out()
```

FIG 1.19: Result of calling a parent's method and overriding it

```
I am a person.
Just kidding. I am not a person.
```

1.9 ENCAPSULATION

The third and final fundamental property of object-oriented programming is **encapsulation**. This property allows programmers to prevent access or alteration to private data, allowing the data to be safe from interference or misuse. Encapsulation can be implemented using the access modifiers mentioned previously: public, protected, and private.

Chapter 2 Data Structures

CHAPTER CONTENTS

2.1 Lists
2.2 Stack
2.3 Queue
2.4 Priority Queue

2.1 LISTS

Arrays are one of the most basic and well known **data structures** in any object-oriented programming language. An array holds a set of values that are of the same data type. Arrays store data in a contiguous fashion within memory, which means that at the creation of an array object, a portion of contiguous memory is allocated to store the array. It is important to note that the "size," or length, of an array is **fixed**. Thus, there is a limit to how many elements can fit in an array. If a programmer attempts to add another element into a full array, an error will occur because there is no memory available to store any more elements.

An array itself is one-dimensional, and its size cannot change. However, in order to use arrays in Python, a library must be imported. Python lists can be used instead. In Python, **lists** are just like arrays, but are dynamic. Lists in Python are not fixed in size as arrays are and are able to contain different data types until arrays. So in Python, we can think of a list as an equivalent to an array, but slightly more powerful.

TRAVERSING A LIST

To **traverse** a list, we take advantage of the indexes provided for us. The following example shows how we can traverse a list and print out the value at each index.

FIG 2.1: Traversing a list and printing out value at each index

```
1    animals = ["cat", "dog", "horse", "bird"]
2
3    # printing out the value at each index of the list
4    for x in animals:
5        print(x)
```

The output would look like the following:

FIG 2.2: Result of traversing a list and printing out the value at each index

We can also traverse lists to assign values to each index.

FIG 2.3: Traversing a list to assign a value to each index

```
1    animal_list = []
2
3    # assigning values to the animal_list
4    for x in range(5):
5        animal_list.append("dog")
6        print(animal_list[x])
```

FIG 2.4: Result of traversing a list to assign value to each index

REMOVING AN ELEMENT FROM A LIST

With a list, we are able to remove a particular element from the list. The method is pop(). If we were to not pass any argument through the method, then the last element of the set would be removed. However, if we pass the index of whatever element through the method, then we are able to remove a targeted element. For instance, if we had a list of "cat", "dog", "shoe", "horse", "bird", and we want to remove the element "shoe" we would find the index to be 2 and pass that through the method. The following shows the implementation of this method.

FIG 2.5: Removing the element at index 2 from a list

```
1    animals = ["cat", "dog", "shoe", "horse", "bird"]
2    animals.pop(2)
3    for x in animals:
4        print(x)
```

FIG 2.6: Results of pop(2) method

2.2 STACK

Another way to store data is through a data structure called a **stack**. A stack is exactly what its name implies: it is a stack of data, similar to a stack of paper or boxes. The following example shows a stack that holds integers 7, 6, and 5.

FIG 2.7: Visual representation of a stack

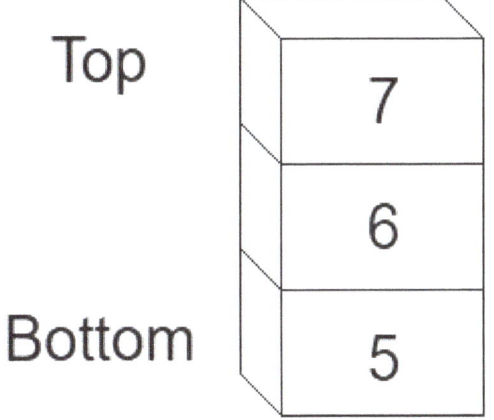

Stack has a "last in, first out" policy, or LIFO, meaning the last item added to the stack will be the first item to get removed. When adding to a stack, you add to the top, and when removing from a stack, you remove from the top.

ADDING AND REMOVING

Our stack in the above example holds three integers. Let's add the integer 8 to the stack. Because stack has a "last in, first out" policy, the added integer will go on top of the stack.

FIG 2.8: *Adding integer 8 to the stack*

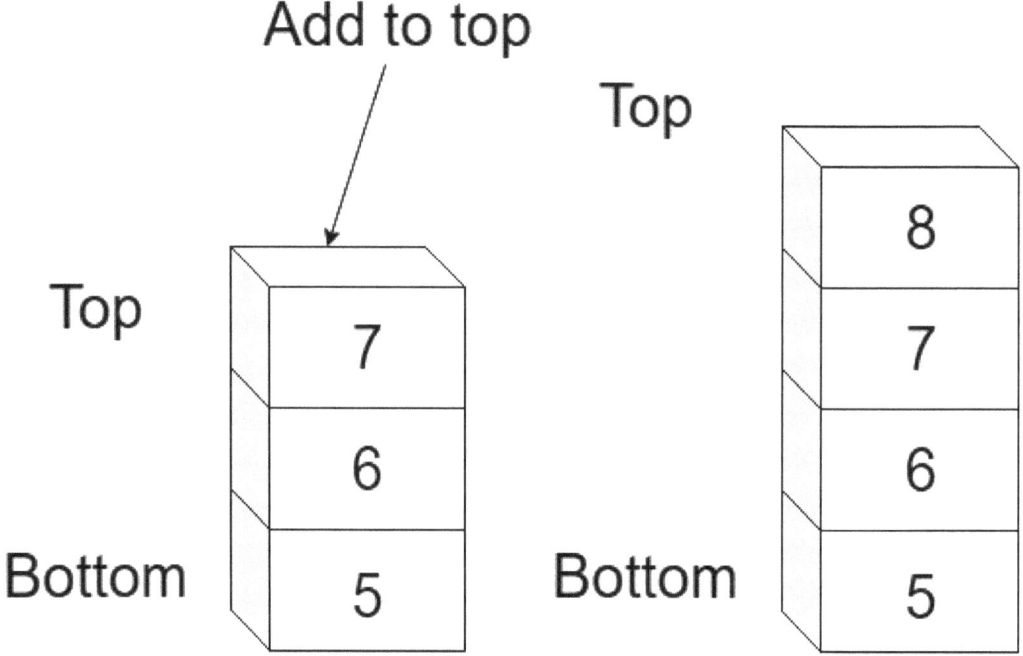

Now, let's remove two integers from our stack.

FIG 2.9: Removing integers 8 and 7 from the stack

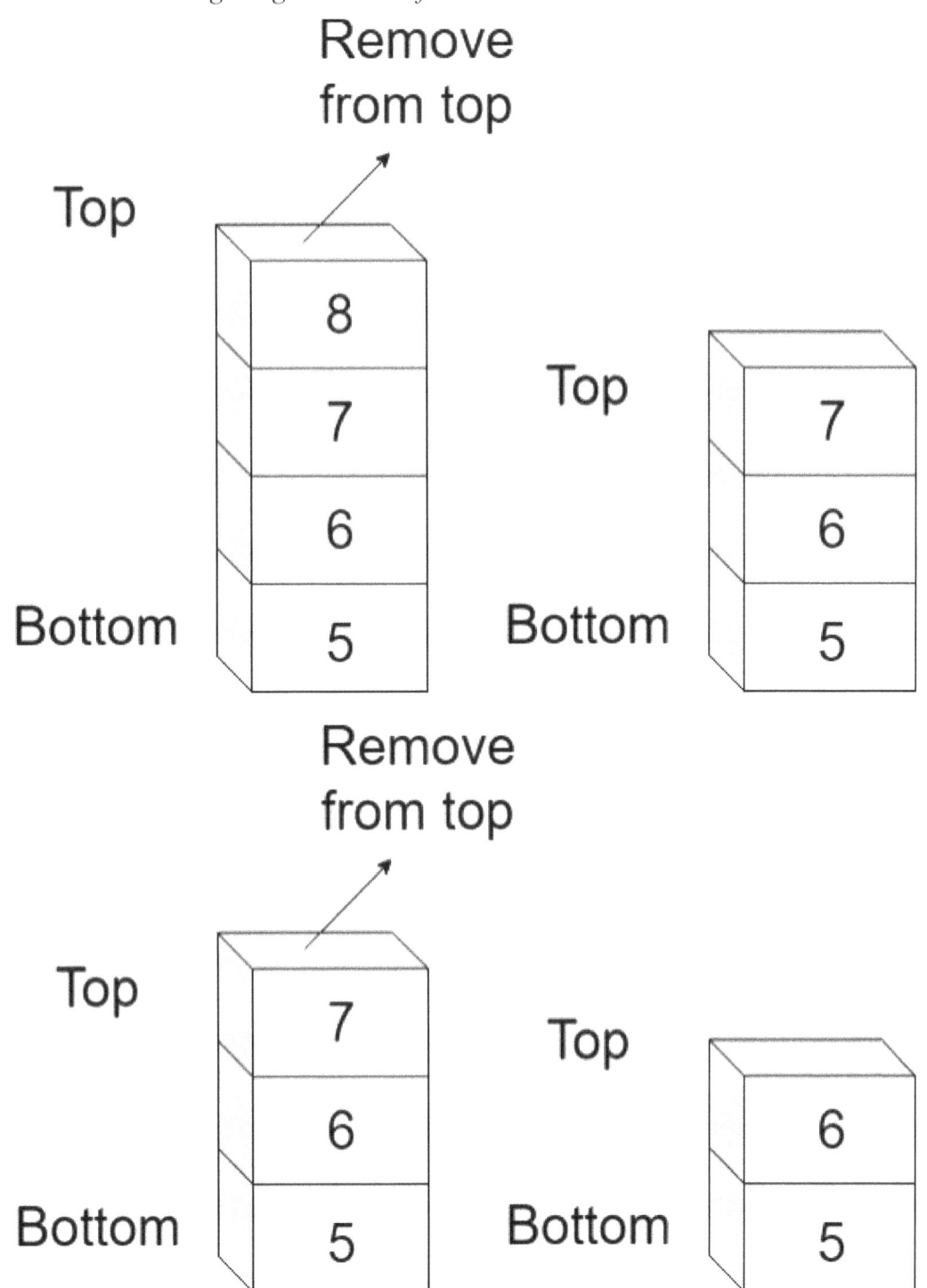

After removing integers 8 and 7 from the stack, we are left with integers 6 and 5.

Stacks can be implemented in different ways. One way in which stacks can be implemented is using lists. In the following example, we'll create a new stack using a list and the methods append and pop to add and remove elements from the stack.

FIG 2.10: Creating an object called stack, adding four integers to the stack, and removing two integers from the stack

```
stack = []

stack.append(5)
stack.append(6)
stack.append(7)
stack.append(8)

stack.pop()
stack.pop()

for x in range(len(stack)):
    print(stack.pop())
```

FIG 2.11: Result of creating a list called stack, adding four integers, removing two integers, then printing the remaining two by removing them.

2.3 QUEUE

Another common data structure is a **queue**. The way a queue works is similar to waiting in line: in the same way that the first person to get in line is the first person to leave, the first element to enter a queue is the first element to leave. If another person wants to get in line, they go to the end of the line. Similarly, added elements will go to the end of a queue. Simply put, a queue has a "first in, first out" policy.

The following example shows a queue that holds the integers 2, 3, and 4.

FIG 2.12: Visual representation of a queue

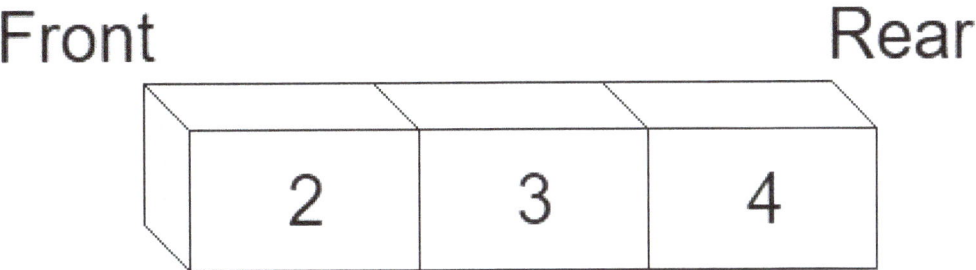

ADDING AND REMOVING

Our queue in the above example holds three integers. Let's add integer 5 to the queue. Because the queue has a "first in, first out" policy, the added integer will go to the end of the queue.

FIG 2.13: Adding integer 5 to the queue

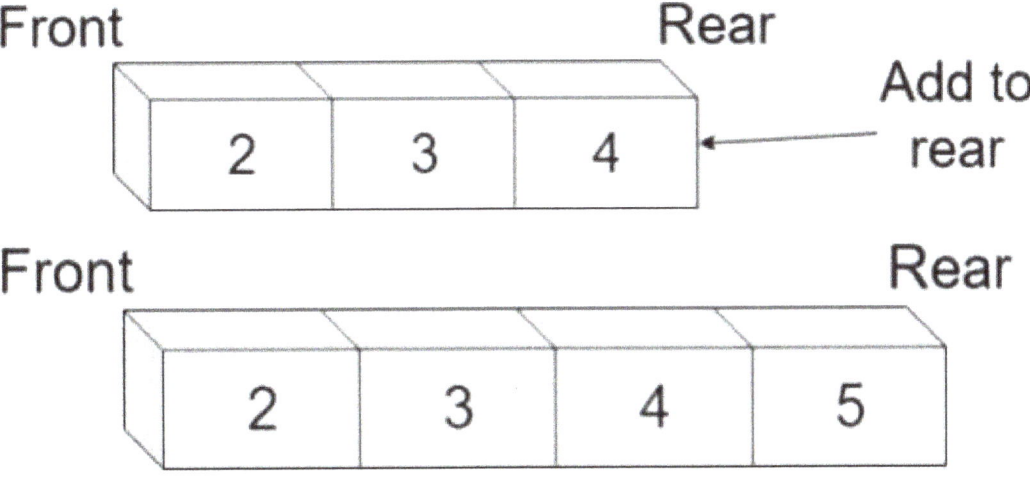

Now let's remove an integer from our queue.

FIG 2.14: Removing integer 2 from the queue

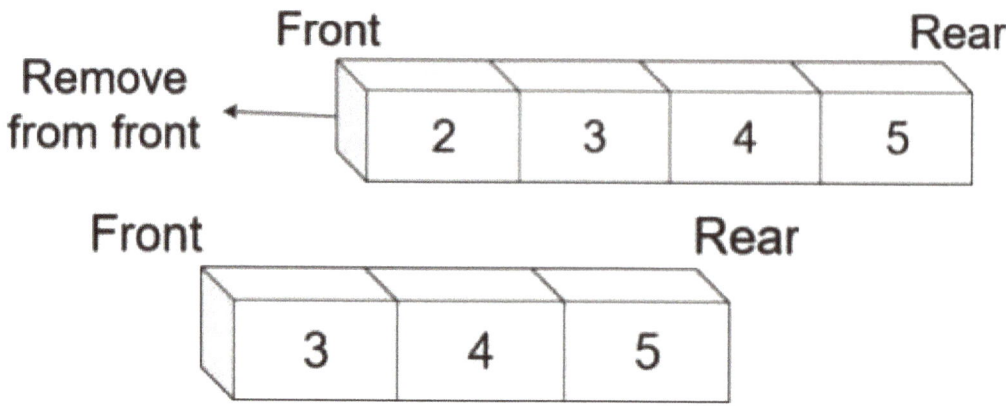

Like stack, queue can be implemented in various ways. The following code shows how queues can be implemented using lists. Elements are added and removed by using the append and pop methods.

FIG 2.15: Creating an object called queue, adding four integers to the queue, and removing an integer from the queue

```
queue = []

queue.append(2)
queue.append(3)
queue.append(4)
queue.append(5)

queue.pop(0)

for x in range(len(queue)):
    print(queue.pop(0))
```

FIG 2.16: Result of creating a list called queue, adding four integers, removing an integer, then printing the remaining three by removing them.

2.4 PRIORITY QUEUE

A special type of data structure that sorts its elements based on **priority** is called a **priority queue.** A priority queue is significantly different from a stack or a queue because in a priority queue, the order in which elements enter the priority queue has no effect on the order of removal of the elements from the priority queue. The order of removal is dictated by the priority of each element added to the queue.

The priority queue in the following example sorts tasks according to their priority. The task with the highest priority is at the front of the queue, whereas the task with the lowest priority is at the end of the queue.

Here's our tasks:

Task	Priority
A	5
B	2
C	3
D	7

Here's the priority queue:

FIG 2.17: Priority queue that sorts tasks according to priority

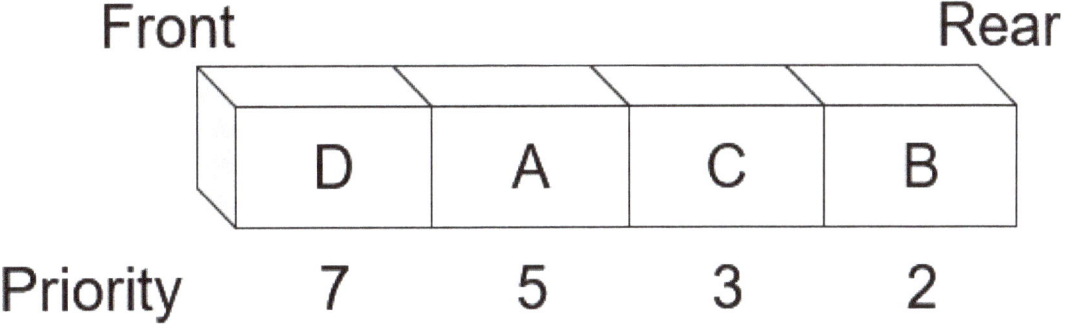

In the above example, task D has the highest priority. Therefore, it is at the front of the priority queue. Task B has the lowest priority, so it is at the end of the priority queue.

ADDING AND REMOVING

Elements are sorted based on priority, not arrival time, so elements that enter a priority queue do not necessarily go to the end. Added elements get sorted into the priority queue so that the entire priority queue remains organized by priority.

Let's add another task to our priority queue.

Task	Priority
A	5
B	2
C	3
D	7
E	9

FIG 2.18: *Adding task to priority queue*

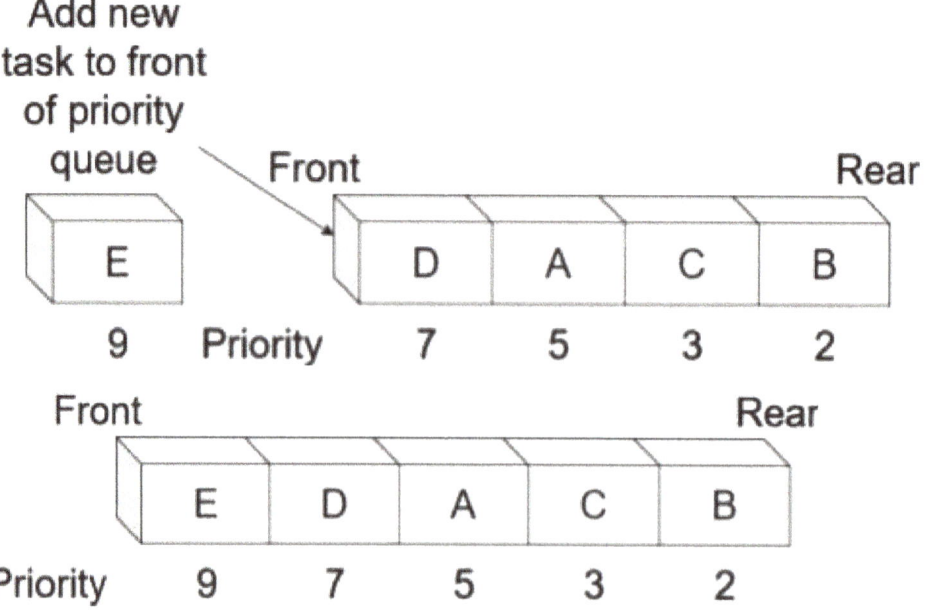

Because the new task, task E, had the highest priority, it got sent to the front of the priority queue.

Let's add another task to our priority queue.

Task	Priority
A	5
B	2
C	3
D	7
E	9
F	4

FIG 2.19: *Adding task to priority queue*

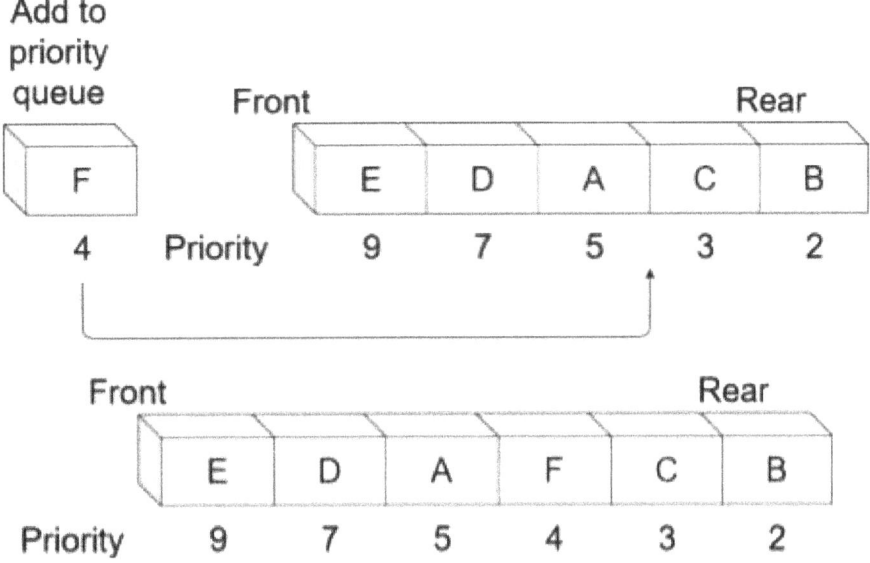

Adding an element to a priority queue may be different from adding an element to a queue, but removing an element from a priority queue is actually quite similar to removing an element from a queue. When removing elements from a priority queue, we remove the element at the front, just like we would in a typical queue. However, it is essential to understand that a priority queue differs from a queue because the first element in a priority queue is not necessarily the first element that entered. Queue has a "first in, first out" policy, and priority queue has a "highest priority, first out" policy.

Let's remove a task from our priority queue. Task E is at the front of the priority queue, so it gets removed.

FIG 2.20: Removing task from priority queue

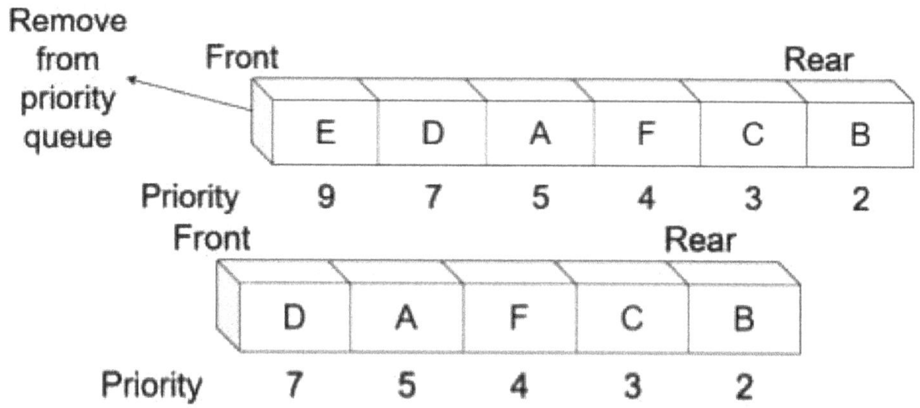

You may be wondering how the priority of an element in a priority queue is determined. The priority of an element is determined by the programmer. For example, a programmer might create a priority queue to dismiss students for lunch based on their test scores. In that case, the students with the highest priority would have good test scores, and the students with the lowest priority would have bad test scores.

Priority queues can be implemented in various ways. The following code shows the implementation of priority queue using the concept of nodes and linked lists.

FIG 2.21: *PriorityQueue class*

```python
class Node:
    def __init__(self, data, priority):
        self.data = data
        self.next = None
        self.priority = priority


class PriorityQueue:
    def __init__(self):
        self.head = None

    def is_empty(self):
        return self.head is None

    # adds the given node to the queue based on priority
    def enqueue(self, data, priority):
        new_node = Node(data, priority)
        prev = self.head
        temp = self.head.next
        if self.is_empty():
            self.head.next = new_node
        else:
            while new_node.priority > temp.priority and temp.next is not None:
                prev = prev.next
                temp = temp.next
            if new_node.priority > temp.priority:
                temp.next = new_node
            else:
                prev.next = new_node
                new_node.next = temp

```

```python
    # removes and returns the data of the node with highest priority
    def dequeue(self):
        if self.is_empty():
            print("Queue is empty")
            return
        temp = self.head
        self.head = self.head.next
        return temp.data
```

Chapter 3: Linked Lists

CHAPTER CONTENTS

3.1 Linked List
3.2 Doubly Linked List

3.1 LINKED LIST

Linked lists are linear, dynamic data structures that are commonly used in object-oriented programming. Linked lists can be manipulated in many ways, with variations including doubly-linked linked lists and circularly linked linked lists. For the purposes of this chapter, we will focus on the implementation of singly-linked linked lists.

Linked lists have **dynamic memory allocation**, meaning memory is allocated at runtime, not immediately as linked lists are constructed. Furthermore, the number of elements in a linked list is not fixed, so linked lists have **dynamic size**. Linked lists can access elements in a linked list by beginning at the first element and **traversing** through the rest of the linked list, element by element. Elements in a linked list cannot be accessed through an index system.

THE NODE CLASS

As stated earlier, a linked list is made up of objects of the class Node. Let's take a closer look at the Node class. Node objects, or **nodes**, hold data and a **reference** to another node. The public variable "data" is the reference to the data the node stores. To access or change the data inside of a node, we can reference the node's "data" variable. The public variable "next" is the reference to the next node in the linked list. The variable "next" is null if there is no reference to another node.

The following example shows a node that holds integer 5. There is no reference to the following node yet, so "next" is null.

FIG 3.1: Node object that holds an integer value of 5

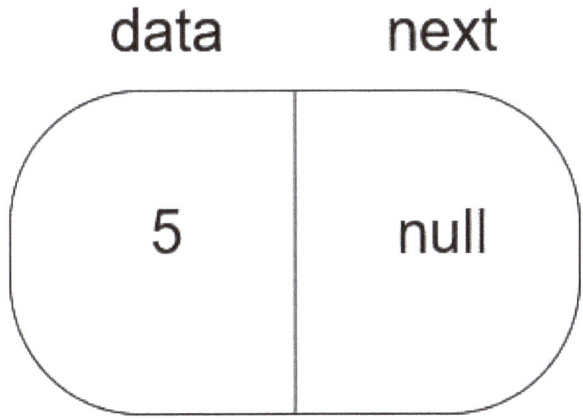

The following is an example of a linked list where each node holds an integer. Each node (except for the last node) in the linked list has a "next" variable that references the next node in the linked list. The last node does not have a reference to another node, so its "next" points to null. Note that head points to the first node in the list. The arrows in the following examples imply a reference to a node. In Python, the keyword "None" is used to represent null objects.

FIG 3.2: A linked list

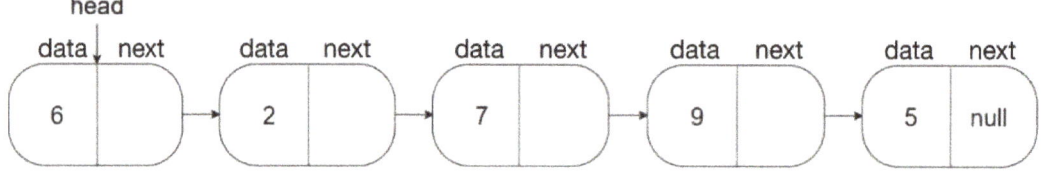

FIG 3.3: The Node class

```
1    class Node(object):
2        def __init__(self, data):
3            self.data = data
4            self.next = None
5
6        def display_node(self):
7            print("Data:", self.data)
```

THE LINKEDLIST CLASS

A **linked list** is an object of the class LinkedList. Linked lists are linked objects of class Node. These objects, commonly known as **nodes**, each hold an element and a **reference**, or link, to the next node in the linked list. The LinkedList class has a reference to only one node: head, which points to the first node in a linked list. The only way to access other elements in a linked list is through **traversal**. The LinkedList class includes methods that can insert elements at the front and back of the linked list, delete elements from the front and back of the linked list, and print the linked list.

FIG 3.4: *The LinkedList class*

```python
class LinkedList:
    def __init__(self):
        self.head = None

    # method that returns whether the list is empty
    def is_empty(self):
        return self.head is None

    # method that inserts an element at the front of the list
    def insert_at_front(self, data):
        new_node = Node(data)
        new_node.next = self.head
        self.head = new_node

    # method that removes the element at the front of the list
    def remove_at_front(self):
        if self.is_empty():
            return
        else:
            self.head = self.head.next
```

```python
        # method that inserts an element at the end of the list
        def insert_at_end(self, data):
            new_node = Node(data)
            if self.is_empty():
                self.head = new_node
            else:
                current = self.head
                while current.next is not None:
                    current = current.next
                current.next = new_node

        # method that removes the element at the end of the list
        def remove_at_end(self):
            if self.is_empty():
                return
            if self.head.next is None:
                self.head = None
            else:
                current = self.head
                while current.next.next is not None:
                    current = current.next
                current.next = None

        # method that returns the list as a string object
        def get_list(self):
            current = self.head
            l_list = None
            while current is not None:
                l_list += current.data
                l_list += ";"
                current = current.next
            return l_list

```

```
64    def display_list(self):
65        current = self.head
66        while current is not None:
67            current.display_node()
68            current = current.next
```

CREATING A LINKED LIST

Now that you have some background on the LinkedList and Node classes, let's try creating a linked list. When creating an object of the LinkedList class, the constructor initializes the variable head as null, signifying that there is nothing at the front of the list. In other words, the linked list starts out empty. Our new instance of LinkedList will be called list, and it will start out empty.

FIG 3.5: *Creating a new object of class LinkedList called linked_list*

```
71    linked_list = LinkedList()
```

Now we've created our LinkedList object.

INSERTING TO THE FRONT OF A LINKED LIST

Right now, our linked list is empty. To add data to our linked list, we can add it to the front. To do so, we must call the insert_at_front method within the LinkedList class. The insert_at_front method creates a new node. In this case, we'll call the node new_node and have it hold integer 5.

FIG 3.6: *Node object new_node that holds integer 5*

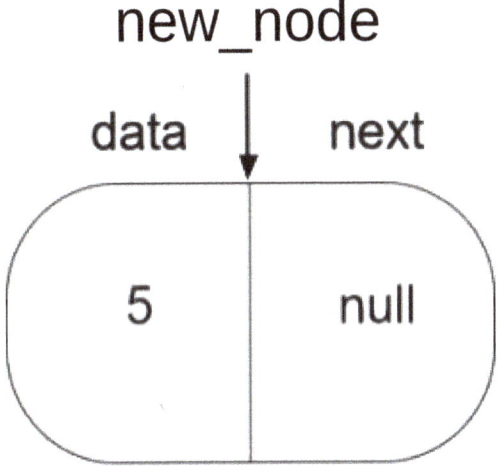

Our node's variable "next" points to null upon construction because there is no reference to another node yet. After the node is created, the insert_at_front method makes new_node's "next" point to head, which points to null in an empty list. Then the method makes head point to the new front of the list, new_node.

FIG 3.7: *Head pointing to the new Node object after the insert_at_front method is completed*

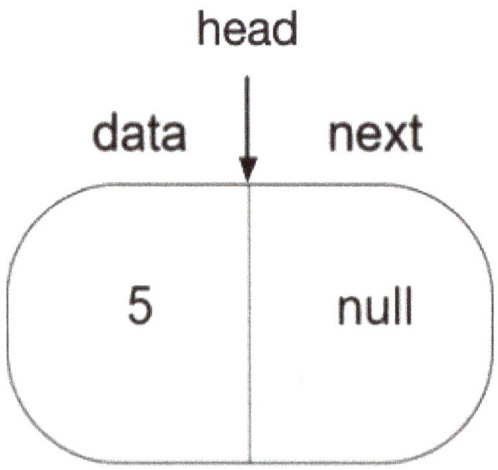

It may seem like we've done a lot, but in reality, this process amounts to adding just one line of code to our driver.

FIG 3.8: *Inserting the integer 5 to the front of a linked list*

```
71      linked_list = LinkedList()
72      linked_list.insert_at_front(5)
```

FIG 3.9: *A closer look at the insert_at_front method inside class LinkedList*

```
19          def insert_at_front(self, data):
20              new_node = Node(data)
21              new_node.next = self.head
22              self.head = new_node
```

Now, let's insert another integer into our linked list. We will add the integer 9 to the front of our list by calling the insert_at_front method. Once again, the method begins with the construction of a new node object called new_node. This time, the node will hold the integer 9.

FIG 3.10: *New node object new_node holding integer 9*

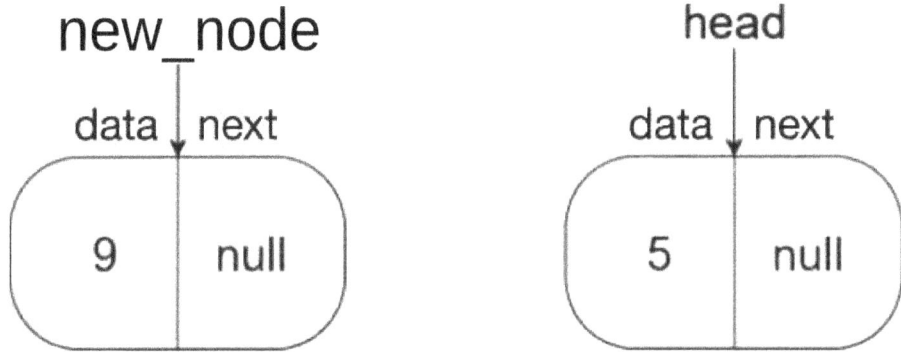

FIG 3.11: *Variable "next" of new_node referencing head*

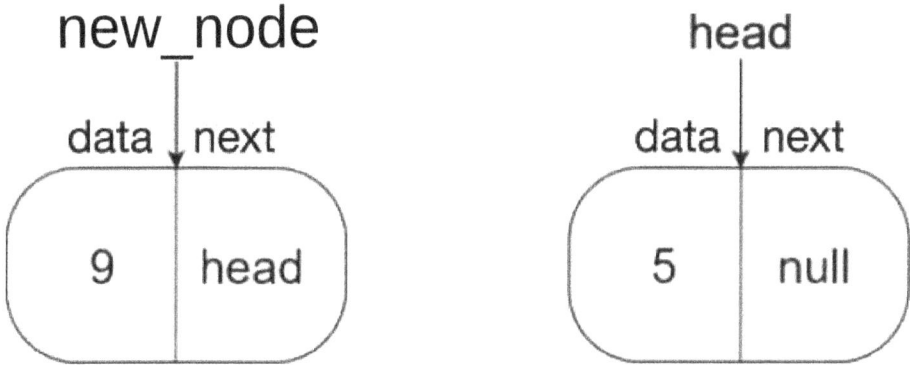

We can also visualize this connection between new_node and head as an arrow that points to head.

FIG 3.12: *Another representation of variable "next" of new_node referencing head*

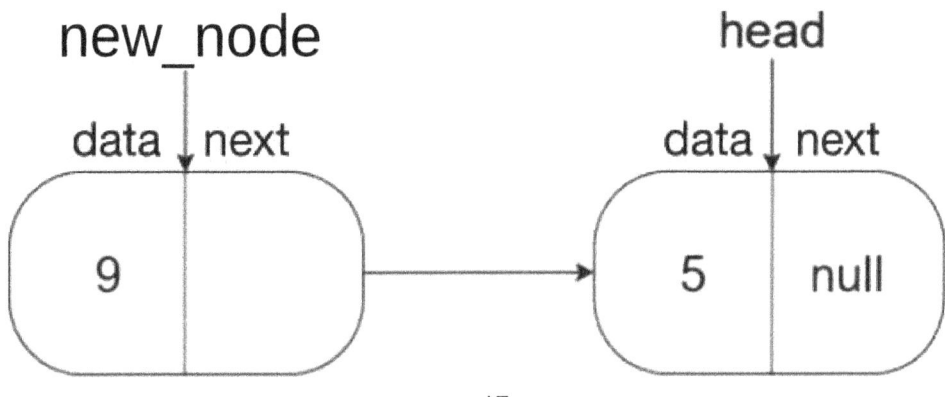

Now that new_node is the new front of the list, we must make head point to new_node.

FIG 3.13: *Head pointing to the new node after the insert_at_front method is completed*

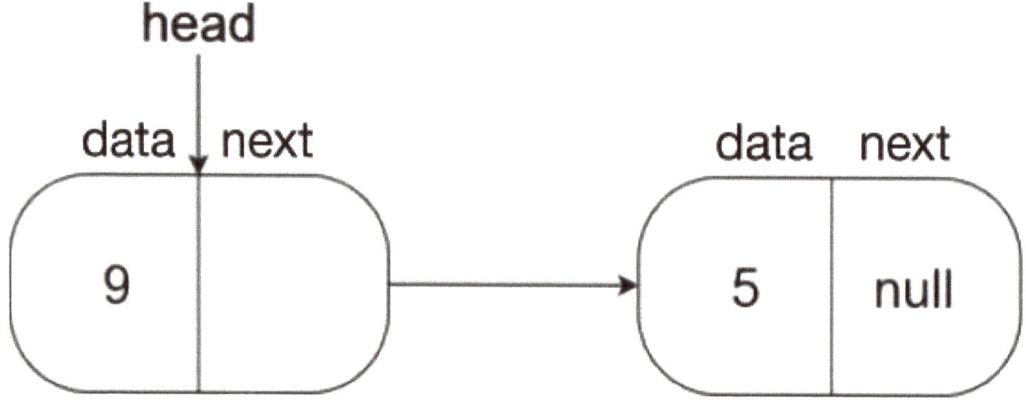

By adding another Node object to our linked list, we've added another line of code to our driver.

FIG 3.14: *Inserting integer 9 to the front of our linked list object*

```
71      linked_list = LinkedList()
72      linked_list.insert_at_front(5)
73      linked_list.insert_at_front(9)
```

The size of our linked list is now 2. Note that there is no longer a direct reference to the node containing integer 5 because head references the first node in our linked list, which contains integer 9. However, the node containing integer 5 is still accessible because the first node has a reference to that object.

TRAVERSING A LINKED LIST

Now that we know how to insert a new node at the front of a linked list, we can create a linked list with several Node objects.

FIG 3.15: *Linked list with several Node objects*

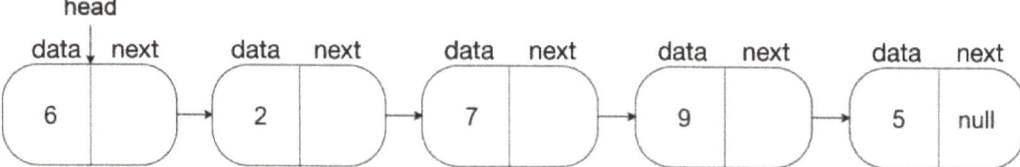

The size of the linked list in the above example is 5 as there are 5 elements in the list. Remember, we do not have any direct references to any of the nodes in the linked list except for the first node, which is referenced by head. This lack of direct references makes it difficult to access data within the linked list or add and delete nodes at the back of the linked list. To access data or add and delete nodes at the end, we must **traverse** the linked list.

To access the last node in a linked list, we would traverse the linked list until we reach the end. A simple algorithm to do this would follow these steps:

1) Check if the linked list is empty
    a) if empty, we cannot traverse the linked list
2) Create a temporary variable to keep track of the current node that is being visited
    a) we do not want to actually change the head accidentally
3) If the current node's "next" variable does not point to null, we can change the temporary variable to be the next node in the list
4) Repeat checking and changing the temporary node until null is reached
    a) we knew were are at the last Node once "next" is null

An implementation of this algorithm might look like the following:

FIG 3.16: *Traversing a linked list until the end is reached*

```
71              # step one: checking if linked list is empty
72              if not self.is_empty():
73                  # step two: creating temporary variable to
        represent current node object being visited
74                  current = self.head
75                  # step three & four: while temporary
        variable's "next" is not none, point "next" to next
        Node object
76                  while current.next is not None:
77                      current = current.next
```

INSERTING TO THE BACK OF A LINKED LIST

Now that we know how to traverse a linked list, we can add to the end of our linked list using the insert_at_end method inside the LinkedList class. Let's add the integer 8 to the back of our linked list. The first step within the method is to create a new node called new_node to hold the data.

FIG 3.17: New node called new_node that holds integer 8

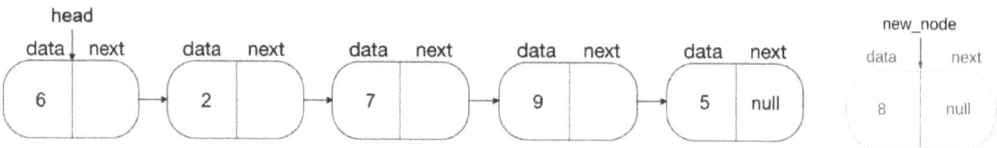

To add new_node to the linked list, the insert_at_end method makes the "next" variable of the last node in the linked list point to new_node. Thus, new_node becomes the new end of the linked list.

FIG 3.18: Variable "next" of last node in linked list referencing new_node

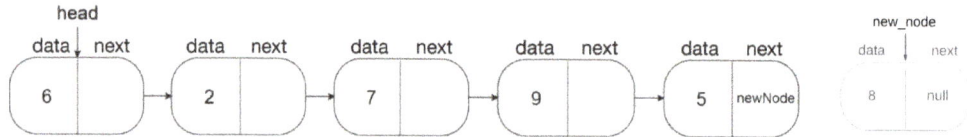

We can also visualize this connection between the last node and new_node as an arrow that points to the new_node.

FIG 3.19: Another representation of variable "next" of last node in linked list referencing new_node

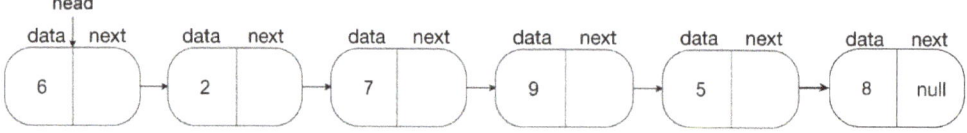

Inserting a new Node object at the end of our linked list required just one additional line of code in our driver. This line of code called method insert_at_end within the LinkedList class.

FIG 3.20: Inserting the integer 8 at the back of our linked list

```
71    linked_list = LinkedList()
72    linked_list.insert_at_front(5)
73    linked_list.insert_at_front(9)
74    linked_list.insert_at_front(7)
75    linked_list.insert_at_front(2)
76    linked_list.insert_at_front(6)
77    linked_list.insert_at_end(8)
```

FIG 3.21: A closer look at the insert_at_end method inside class LinkedList

```
    def insert_at_end(self, data):
        new_node = Node(data)
        if self.is_empty():
            self.head = new_node
        else:
            current = self.head
            while current.next is not None:
                current = current.next
            current.next = new_node
```

DELETING FROM THE FRONT OF A LINKED LIST

To remove a value from a linked list, we must remove the reference to the node holding that value. The node will still exist in memory, but there will be no way to access it. It is imperative to delete values from a linked list correctly because if a reference to any node is lost, it is impossible to access that node or the nodes that come after it.

So how do we remove the reference to a node to delete a value from a linked list? If we want to remove the node at the front of the list, for example, we would simply make head point to the next object in the list. If there is not another object in the list, head would then point to null.

In the following example, we will remove the reference to the first node in a linked list with 5 nodes.

FIG 3.22: Linked list with 5 Node objects

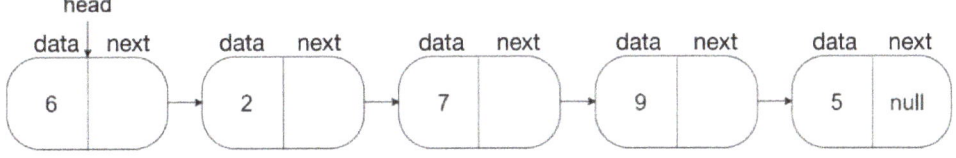

FIG 3.23: Making head point to the second node in the linked list

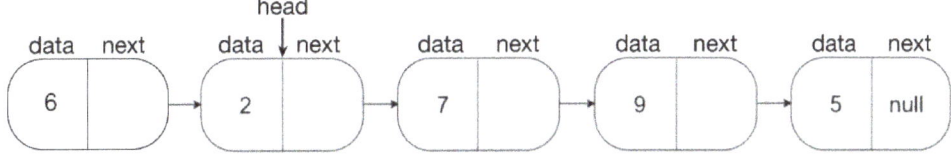

Even though the node before the new head still exists, there is no way to access it. Therefore, we consider it "deleted."

FIG 3.24: *Result of "deleting" the first node in a linked list*

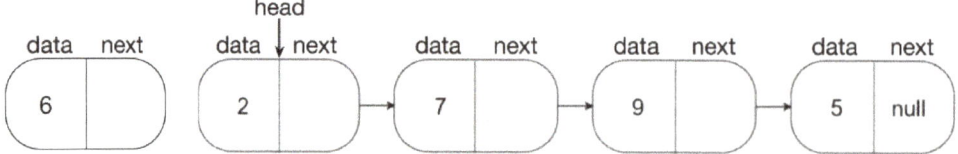

Removing a Node object at the front of our linked list required just one additional line of code in our driver. This line of code called the method remove_at_front within the LinkedList class.

FIG 3.25: *Removing at the front of a linked list*

```
71    linked_list = LinkedList()
72    linked_list.insert_at_front(5)
73    linked_list.insert_at_front(9)
74    linked_list.insert_at_front(7)
75    linked_list.insert_at_front(2)
76    linked_list.insert_at_front(6)
77    linked_list.remove_at_front()
```

Here's the method used to remove the node at the front of a linked list:

FIG 3.26: *Method remove_at_front inside class LinkedList that removes node at front of linked list*

```
25        def remove_at_front(self):
26            if self.is_empty():
27                return
28            else:
29                self.head = self.head.next
```

DELETING FROM THE BACK OF A LINKED LIST

Deleting from the back of a linked list is similar to deleting from the front of a linked list. We must remove the reference to the node at the end of the list. To do so, we first check if the linked list is empty or only has one node. If the linked list is empty, we do nothing. If the linked list has only one node, we make the head point to null instead of the first node. If there is more than one node, we must traverse to the second-to-last node in the list and make its variable "next" point to null.

In the following example, we will remove the reference to the last node in a linked list with 5 nodes.

FIG 3.27: *Linked list with 5 nodes*

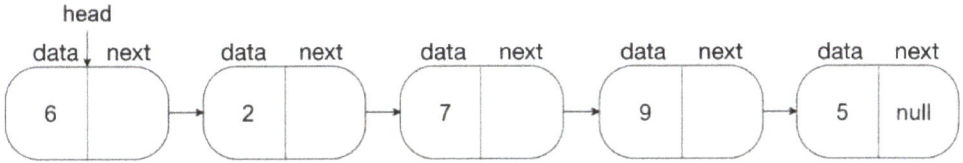

FIG 3.28: *Making the second-to-last node's variable "next" point to null*

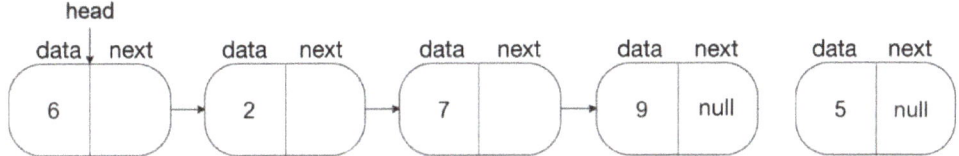

Removing a Node object at the end of our linked list required just one additional line of code in our driver. This line of code calls the method remove_at_end within the LinkedList class.

FIG 3.29: *Removing at the end of a linked list*

```
71      linked_list = LinkedList()
72      linked_list.insert_at_front(5)
73      linked_list.insert_at_front(9)
74      linked_list.insert_at_front(7)
75      linked_list.insert_at_front(2)
76      linked_list.insert_at_front(6)
77      linked_list.remove_at_end()
```

Here's the method used to remove the node at the end of a linked list:

FIG 3.30: *Method remove_at_end inside class LinkedList that removes the last node of a linked list*

```
43      def remove_at_end(self):
44          if self.is_empty():
45              return
46          if self.head.next is None:
47              self.head = None
48          else:
49              current = self.head
50              while current.next.next is not None:
51                  current = current.next
52              current.next = None
```

CIRCULAR LINKED LIST

Understanding the ins and outs of a singular linked list allows you to take a small step towards Circular Linked List. Now, instead of having the value of "next" for the final node point to null, we can connect the final node to the first node of the list. The list is now like a rubber band. If an ant were to talk on the surface of a rubber band, it would eventually traverse the entire band and return to its original position. In the same vein, you are able to return to the head of the linked list by simply continuing to travel forwards. That is achieved by simply changing the "next" value of the last node to point to the first node.

3.2 DOUBLY LINKED LIST

Adding the adverb, doubly, in front of linked list does not mean it is twice as difficult to understand. As mentioned before, each node in a linked list has two attributes: an element and a reference to the next node. In a doubly linked list, each node has three attributes: an element, a reference to the next node, and a reference to the previous node. As a result, we are able to traverse through the linked list in two directions. Since each node has a link to the previous nodes, certain methods are slightly different for manipulating nodes.

THE NODE CLASS FOR DOUBLY LINKED LIST

Creating a node class for a doubly linked list would only require the addition of one more attribute to the node. Along with the public variable "data" and the public variable "next", we must add the public variable "prev". The new variable "prev" will be the link between the current node and the previous. For the following, the node contains the integer 5. As there are no references to a node before or after, both "prev" and "next" are null.

FIG 3.31: Creating a node with data of 5

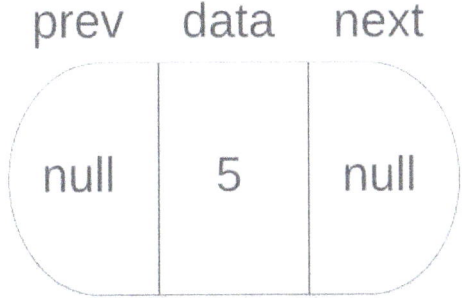

Connecting these nodes with three attributes creates a doubly linked list in which nodes are able to point back to the previous node. Only the "prev" of the head does not point to another node before and is thus null. Similar to a regular linked list, the last node does not have a reference to another node and its "next" points to null. To allow us to traverse backwards in the list, the last node will have a tail. We can treat it like a head and allows us to go from the last node to the first making removing the last node much easier. However, the tail does require more memory as a tradeoff. We would need to keep track of the tail in a similar fashion to how we keep track of the head. The arrows imply a reference to another node.

FIG 3.32: Connecting nodes into a doubly linked list

FIG 3.33: Node class for a doubly linked list

```
class Node(object):
    def __init__(self, data):
        self.data = data
        self.next = None
        self.prev = None
```

CREATING A DOUBLY LINKED LIST

With this new Node class, creating a doubly linked list object is very similar to creating a regular linked list object. The constructor will initialize the variable head as null meaning the list starts empty and tail will be empty as well. We will call our object DoubleLinkedList.

FIG 3.34: *DoublyLinkedList class*

```
11      class DoublyLinkedList:
12          def __init__(self):
13              self.head = None
14              self.tail = None
```

INSERTING AFTER NODE N

Inserting a node at the front and end of a doubly linked list is nearly identical to doing so in a regular linked list. However, keep in mind that we must treat the tail like another head. So adding a node to the end would require us to move the tail to point to the new final node. While that is an easy addition that is not difficult to implement, adding a new node after a node requires slightly more to be done. For example, let's say that we have an existing doubly linked list that contains the following integers: 2, 5, 9, 6.

FIG 3.35: *Existing doubly linked list with data: 2, 5, 9, 6*

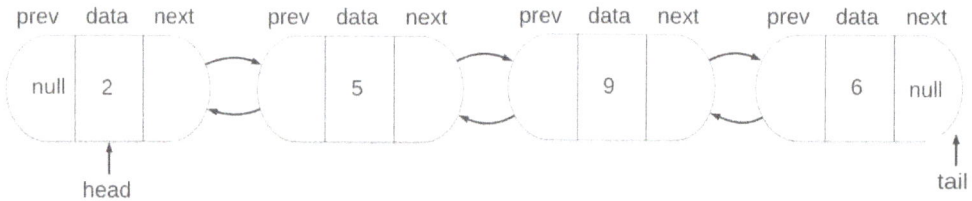

Let's create a method called insert_after that will allow us to create a node of a desired data and add if after a given node, n. In the following example, insert_after will first create a node called new_node that will hold the integer 7 with "next" and "prev" pointing to null.

FIG 3.36: *Creating new_node holding the integer 7*

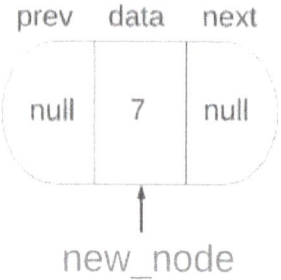

With the given index of where we want to insert the new_node after, we must traverse through the doubly linked list to reach the location. Once we have found the location, the two links between node, n, and the following node, n2, must be broken. The "next" of node, n, must be changed to point to new_node and "prev" of n2 must be changed to point to new_node. As well, "prev" of new_node must point to n and "next" of new_node must point to n2. For this example, we will say that we want to insert new_node after node with index 2. This process is shown below.

FIG 3.37: *Process of insert_after method*

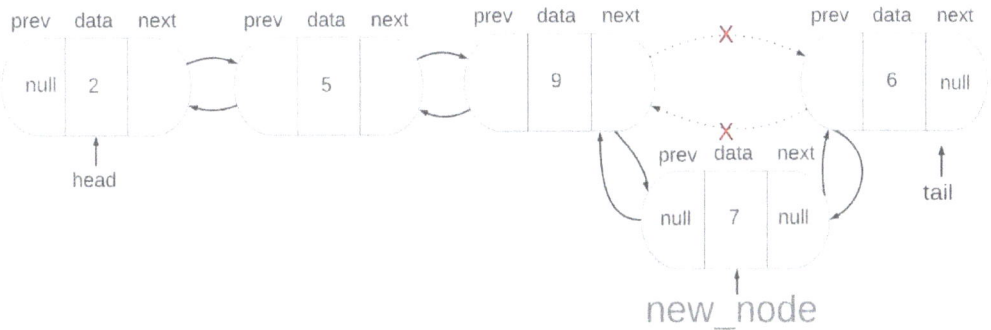

In essence, we will change where the links point to add another node. Once the process is completed, new_node should be entered after index 2. The completed doubly linked list will look as follows.

FIG 3.38: *Results of insert_after method*

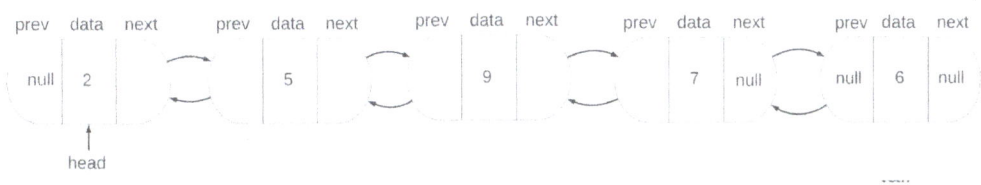

We must check, however, if we are inserting a node at the end of the list. If we were, then the tail must simply be changed to point to the new end last node that was inserted. Method insert_after will be inside the class for DoublyLinkedList.

FIG 3.39: *Inserting 7 after 9*

```
80    d_l_list = DoublyLinkedList()
81    d_l_list.insert_at_front(6)
82    d_l_list.insert_at_front(9)
83    d_l_list.insert_at_front(5)
84    d_l_list.insert_at_front(2)
85    d_l_list.insert_after(d_l_list.head.next.next, 7)
```

FIG 3.40: *insert_after method inside DoublyLinkedList class*

```
61        # method that inserts an element after a known element
62        def insert_after(self, prev_node, data):
63            if prev_node is not None:
64                new_node = Node(data)
65                new_node.next = prev_node.next
66                prev_node.next = new_node
67                new_node.prev = prev_node
68                if new_node.next is not None:
69                    new_node.next.prev = new_node
70                else:
71                    self.tail = new_node
```

REMOVE DATA

To remove a given data from a doubly linked list will still require us to traverse the linked list to find the particular node that contains the data. To best explain this remove_data method, we see how we can move a given data from an already existing list. Let's have a doubly linked list that contains the following integers: 2, 5, 9, 7, 6. We want to remove the number 7 from the list.

FIG 3.41: *Existing doubly linked class with following data: 2, 5, 9, 7, 6*

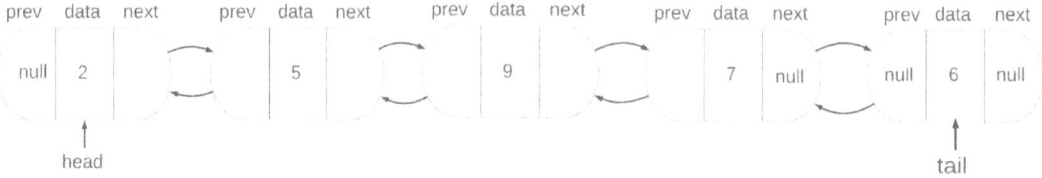

The method remove_data will create a temporary variable called current to keep track of which node we are at. While the data of whatever the current node we are at is not equal to the data we are trying to remove, we will continue to traverse the list. So, we are moving down the list checking each node to see if it holds the data we are looking for. In this instance we are searching for 7 which happens to be at the node with index 3.

FIG 3.42: *remove_data method finding the node holding the desired data we want to remove*

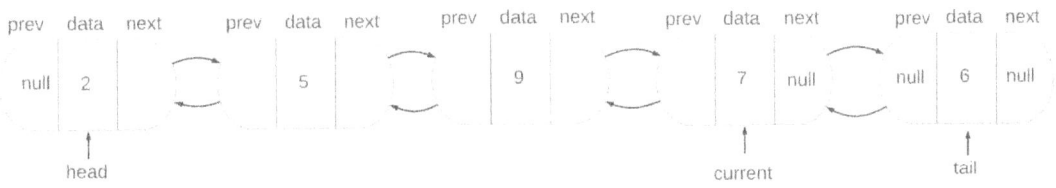

Now that we have found the node we cant to remove, we sever the connection with the existing list. The previous node and next node will be linked together in the following process.

FIG 3.43: *Process of remove_data method*

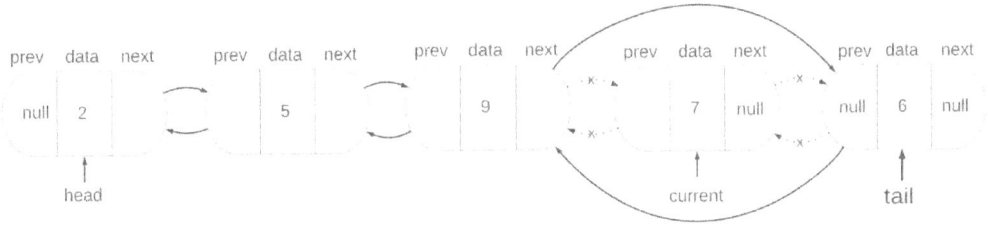

Once the process is completed, our doubly linked list will look as follows without the data 7.

FIG 3.44: *Results of the remove_data method*

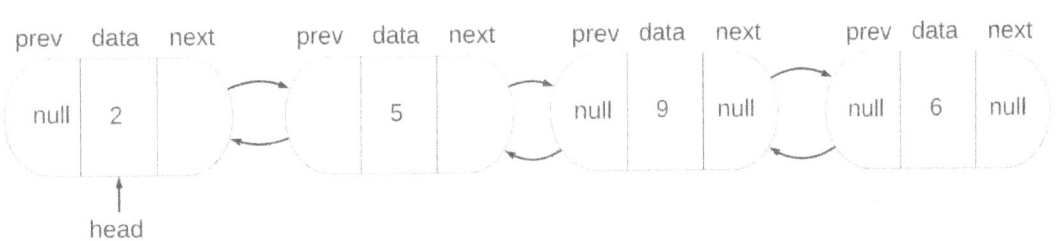

Implementing this method would look like the following:

FIG 3.45: *Removing 7*

```
 98     d_l_list = DoublyLinkedList()
 99     d_l_list.insert_at_front(6)
100     d_l_list.insert_at_front(9)
101     d_l_list.insert_at_front(5)
102     d_l_list.insert_at_front(2)
103     d_l_list.insert_after(d_l_list.head.next.next, 7)
104     d_l_list.remove_data(7)
```

FIG 3.46: *remove_data method in the DoublyLinkedList class*

```
73          # method that removes an element
74          def remove_data(self, data):
75              if self.is_empty():
76                  return
77              if self.head.data == data:
78                  self.head = self.head.next
79              else:
80                  current = self.head
81                  while current is not None and current.data != data:
82                      current = current.next
83                  if current is None:
84                      return
85                  if current.next is None:
86                      current.next.prev = current.prev
87                  else:
88                      self.tail = current.prev
89                  current.prev.next = current.next
```

We had mentioned how the tail is useful for allowing us to traverse backwards from the end of a doubly linked list. However, as you can see from the methods we have implemented, a tail is not always required. Besides changing where the tail points when inserting a new node, it was not helpful in these cases. It is still beneficial to have a tail for a doubly linked list, and as a result nearly 99% of the time a tail will be included.

Chapter 4 Recursion

CHAPTER CONTENTS

4.1 Introduction: Recursion
4.2 Recursion
4.3 Why Recursion?
4.4 Word Break

4.1 INTRODUCTION: RECURSION

In this chapter, we will cover a way to simplify a problem by repeating an action. This is referred to as **recursion**. In simple terms, recursion is the act of a method calling itself until a problem is simplified down to a **base case**. Recursion makes it easy to solve certain problems as the problem essentially simplifies itself one step at a time.

4.2 RECURSION

To write a recursive method, **if statements** and **else statements** must be used. The if statement usually represents the **base case**, or the smallest, most simple version of the problem. The base case can be thought of as an initial value which is already known. Once the base case is reached, the recursive method stops calling itself.

The else statement is typically the structure that contains operations that help simplify the problem to bring it closer to the base case. The else statement also calls the method within itself, which is the key to recursion. The operations within the else statement will be executed repeatedly until the problem is simplified down to its base case.

If statements and else statements are the basic necessities for writing recursive methods, but it's important to understand that a more complex problem will require recursion with many complex components. For example, it may become necessary in the else statement to execute certain commands before and after the recursive call.

The concept of recursion may seem complex, but an example will help illustrate what exactly a recursive method does. One common example used to demonstrate recursion is a factorial, represented in mathematics with an exclamation point (!). If you are unfamiliar with this notation, a factorial signifies that you multiply the given number by all positive integers less than it. For example, 5! = 5 x 4 x 3 x 2 x 1 = 120. Using the iterative style that you are probably familiar with, calculating a factorial would look like the following:

FIG 4.1: *Calculating factorials with iteration*

```
1    def factorial(n):
2        result = 1
3        for x in range(1, n+1):
4            result *= x
5        return result
6
7
8    print(factorial(5))
```

FIG 4.2: *Result of calculating factorials with iteration*

This problem can be done in a different way using recursion instead of iteration. We know that the base case of a factorial is always 0! = 1. We also know that the factorial of a number is just itself multiplied by the previous number's factorial; in other words, n! = n x (n-1)! Using these two pieces of information, the factorial method can be rewritten using recursion.

FIG 4.3: *Calculating factorials with recursion*

```
1    # calculating n! with recursion
2    def factorial(n):
3        # base case
4        if n == 0:
5            return 1
6        else:
7            # n! = n * (n - 1)!
8            return n * factorial(n - 1)
9
10
11   print(factorial(5))
```

FIG 4.4: *Result of calculating factorials with recursion*

4.3 WHY RECURSION?

In the previous example, it may not be clear why anyone would want to use recursion. A factorial is simple enough that neither recursion nor iteration seems easier or more efficient than the other. However, there are some complicated problems that are extremely difficult or almost impossible without recursion. In the next example, it becomes evident that recursion can simplify a complex problem down to a very simple solution.

Towers of Hanoi is a classic game used to demonstrate the power of recursion. The premise is simple: given a stack of rings of increasing size (see figure 2.5), how can all the rings be transported from tower A to tower C? Only one ring can be moved at a time, and at no point can a larger ring be placed on top of a smaller ring.

FIG 4.5: *Towers of Hanoi*

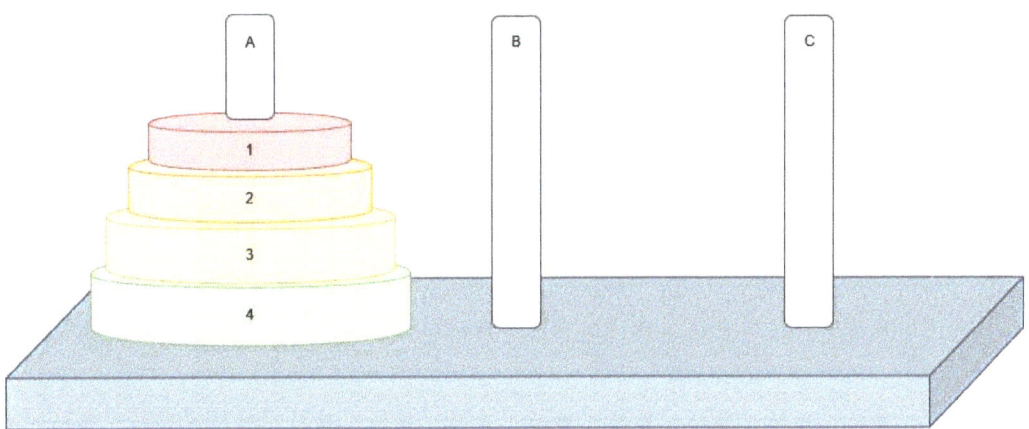

While this problem may seem complicated at first, we can break it down into smaller steps that can then be implemented using recursion. Let's start with finding a solution when there are only two rings.

FIG 4.6: Towers of Hanoi with 2 rings

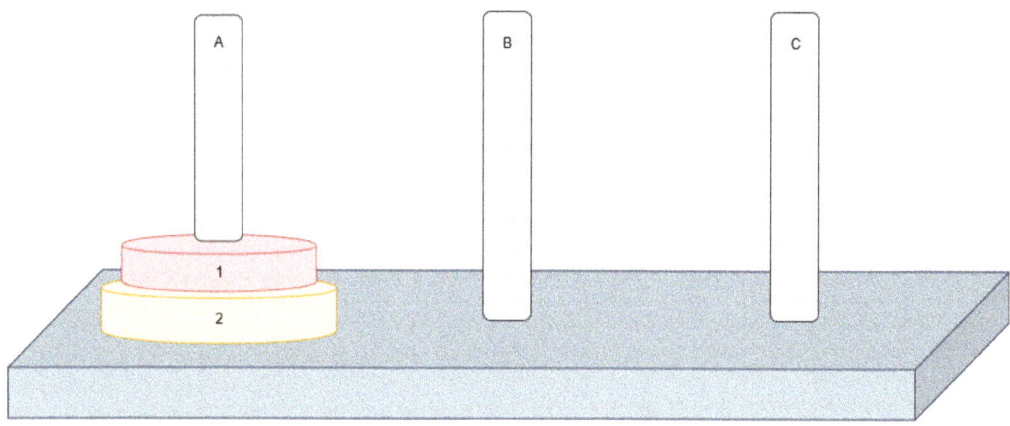

To solve this problem, you would move ring 1 to tower B, then move ring 2 to tower C. Finally, you'd move ring 1 to tower C on top of ring 2. Finding a solution with two rings is simple, and can be accomplished in three moves.

When there are more rings involved, the solution is not as simple. Now, let's try an example where there are three rings instead of 2.

FIG 4.7: Towers of Hanoi with 3 rings

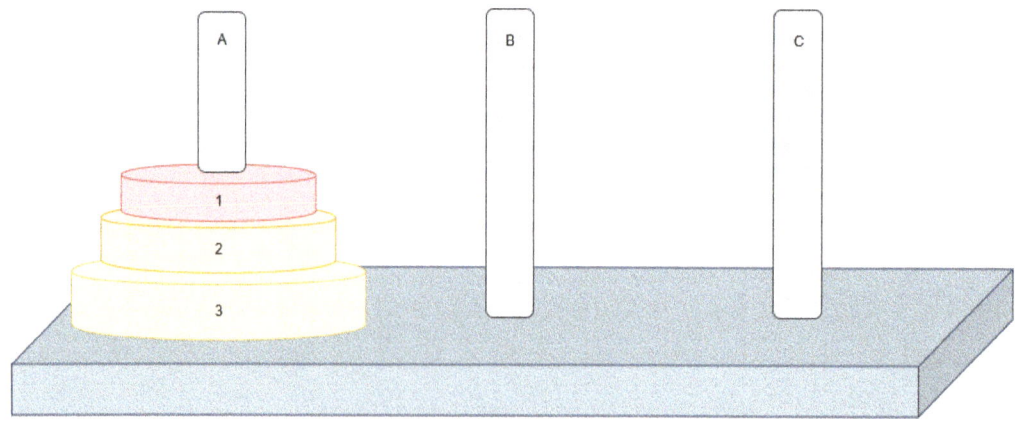

You can use the same strategy from figure 2.6: move rings 1 and 2 to tower B, then move ring 3 to tower C. Finally, move rings 1 and 2 to tower C on top of ring 3. At first glance, it may seem like this approach breaks the rules. After all, rings 1 and 2 cannot be moved together since you can only move one ring at a time. However, recall that we already found a solution for moving rings 1 and 2 from tower A to tower C. This solution can be used here to move rings 1 and 2 from tower A to tower B, then again to move them from tower B to tower C.

If we had 4 rings, the same technique would apply. You would first move rings 1-3 to tower B, then move ring 4 to tower C. Then you'd move rings 1-3 to tower C on top of ring 4.

The implementation of this solution in Python might look something like this:

FIG 4.8: *Solving the Towers of Hanoi problem with recursion*

```python
# n: number of rings
# start: tower that the ring starts on
# extra: the extra tower that isn't the start or the
 target
# target: the tower that the rings should end on


def tower_of_hanoi(n, start, target, extra):
    # base case
    if n == 1:
        # move the ring to the target tower
        print("Move ring 1 from tower", start, "to tower", target)
        return
    else:
        # move the rings above the largest onto the extra tower
        tower_of_hanoi(n - 1, start, extra, target)
        # move the largest onto the target
        print("Move ring", n, "from tower", start, "to tower", target)
        # move the other rings from the extra tower to the target
        tower_of_hanoi(n - 1, extra, target, start)


tower_of_hanoi(4, "A", "C", "B")
```

FIG 4.9: *Result of solving the Towers of Hanoi problem with recursion*

```
Move ring 1 from tower A to tower B
Move ring 2 from tower A to tower C
Move ring 1 from tower B to tower C
Move ring 3 from tower A to tower B
Move ring 1 from tower C to tower A
Move ring 2 from tower C to tower B
Move ring 1 from tower A to tower B
Move ring 4 from tower A to tower C
Move ring 1 from tower B to tower C
Move ring 2 from tower B to tower A
Move ring 1 from tower C to tower A
Move ring 3 from tower B to tower C
Move ring 1 from tower A to tower B
Move ring 2 from tower A to tower C
Move ring 1 from tower B to tower C
```

Even though it may seem like a complicated problem at first, taking the time to break it down and think about it logically results in a solution that is actually quite simple. This particular problem can still be solved with an iterative solution, but it would require more sophisticated data structures and methods. Recursion completes the task in about 30 lines of code.

4.4 WORD BREAK

With our knowledge of recursive, let's examine another instance in which recursive helps break down a given problem. In the Word Break Problem, we will once again demonstrate the necessity of recursion. Say we have a dictionary that contains just three word strings: "in", "to", and "into". Think of our dictionary as a word bank of words that we have and can use for this problem. Now we are given a string: "into". We are asked to recreate the string with the words in our dictionary. As a human, it is easy to recognize the individual words and say:

"into" = "in" + "to"

"into" = "into"

We recreated the string from our dictionary. However, a computer is not able to understand heuristically like a human, and cannot differentiate words. So, for a computer to be able to break down string or sentence, we must use recursive. We will create an algorithm that will examine each prefix and connect it to suffixes and check if that exists in the dictionary. The base case will be if the string is empty so just "". The following diagram expresses how the algorithm would break it down the string for suffixes.

FIG 4.10: *Recursive Tree for WordBreak*

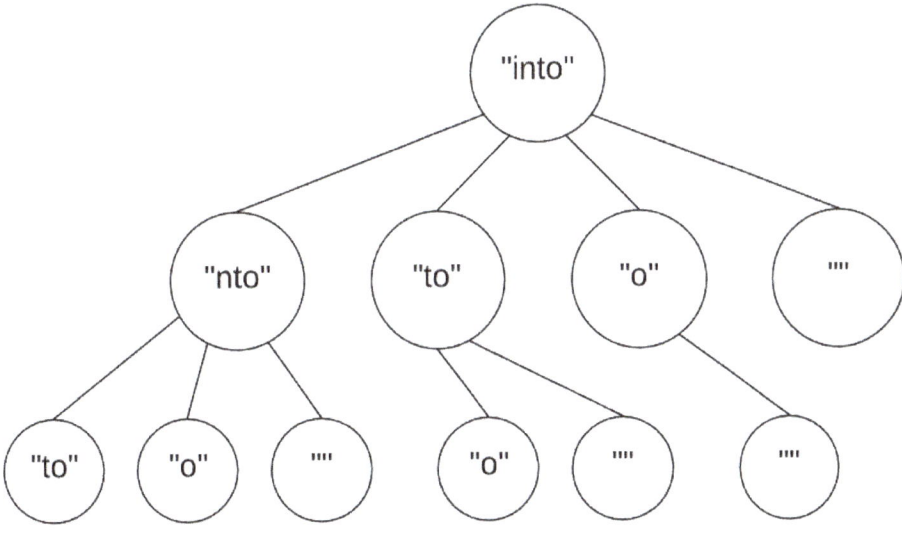

To understand how this tree works, let's look at the bottom left most node that contains "to". In this tree, "to" is the suffix that will be added to the back of the prefix "in". Since the algorithm sees that "in" + "to" = "into", it will check if prefix and suffix in this instance exists in the dictionary. Since it does, the algorithm knows that it has correctly broken down the string.

Now if you were to travel to the parent node which contains the suffix "nto", the prefix "i". Once again, the algorithm sees that "i" + "nto" = "into"; however, neither "i" nor "nto" exists in the dictionary. Thus, the algorithm knows that this is not a valid way of breaking the string.

Now lets implement the method for this example and see what the output is.

FIG 4.11: *Implementing "into" example*

```
def string_traverse(dict, str, output):
    if len(str) == 0:
        print(output)
        return
    for x in range(1, len(str) + 1):
        prefix = str[0:x]
        if prefix in dictionary:
            string_traverse(dict, str[x:], output + " " + prefix)


dictionary = ["in", "to", "into"]
string = "into"
string_traverse(dictionary, string, " ")
```

FIG 4.12: *Output of word break for "into"*

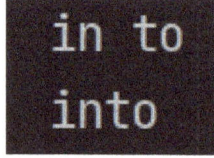

Now that we understand the algorithm, let's see the output for a larger string. This time, we are given a dictionary and asked to break down the string of the following:

Dictionary: {"high", "school", "2019", "summer", "internship", "2020", "is", "the", "best", "intern", "ship", "2", 0", "9", "student"}

String: {"highschoolsummerinternship2020isthebest"}

FIG 4.13 Implementing Word Break

```python
def string_traverse(dict, str, output):
    if len(str) == 0:
        print(output)
        return
    for x in range(1, len(str) + 1):
        prefix = str[0:x]
        if prefix in dictionary:
            string_traverse(dict, str[x:], output + " " + prefix)


dictionary = ["high", "school", "2019", "summer",
    "internship", "2020", "is", "the", "best", "intern",
    "ship", "2", "0", "9", "student"]
string = "highschoolsummerinternship2020isthebest"
string_traverse(dictionary, string, " ")
```

This time the given string is an entire sentence without any spaces between the words. Placing it through the same algorithm we get an output of:

FIG 4.14: Output of word break problem

```
high school summer intern ship 2 0 2 0 is the best
high school summer intern ship 2020 is the best
high school summer internship 2 0 2 0 is the best
high school summer internship 2020 is the best
```

Using recursive, we were able to solve this Word Break Problem simply. It would be nearly impossible to do so without recursion and while it is a difficult concept to understand, once you are able to see the beauty of it you will be able to harness the power effectively.

Chapter 5 Sorting

CHAPTER CONTENTS

5.1 Introduction: Sorting
5.2 Selection Sort
5.3 Insertion Sort
5.4 Bubble Sort
5.5 Quick Sort
5.6 Merge Sort

5.1 INTRODUCTION: SORTING

Have you ever wondered how we can store data in ascending or descending order? As it turns out, there are several methods we can use to go about sorting data. In this chapter, we will focus on four sorting methods: **selection sort, insertion sort, bubble sort,** and **quick sort**.

5.2 SELECTION SORT

Selection Sort is fairly simple to understand. It is able to sort through an array by going over an array over and over, each time placing the smallest element found into the beginning. What is happening is an array is being divided into two subarrays: sorted and unsorted. At the beginning the entire array is unsorted. After a single pass through the entire array, the lowest element is moved to the sorted array at the front. Let's look at an example array to better understand the concept. Here is an array of 5 integers.

Index #	0	1	2	3	4
Value	2	10	8	15	1

Right now the entire array is unsorted. We will indicate that the unsorted subarray in red and the sorted sub array as blue. Updating our array to follow our color code is as follows.

Index #	0	1	2	3	4
Value	2	10	8	15	1

The number of passes we must go through the array is equal to the number of elements in the array. For this example, we will pass through the array 5 times. In the first pass, the smallest value is 1 at index 4.

Index #	0	1	2	3	4
Value	2	10	8	15	1

↑ min

Thus, we will swap index 4 with the first element, index 0, to begin our sorted array.

Index #	0	1	2	3	4
Value	1	10	8	15	2

It is the second pass now and we find the minimum value to be 2 at index 4. Since we now have a sub array for sorted elements created, we now want to enter 2 at the end of our sub array. In this case, we are switching index 1 and 4.

Index #	0	1	2	3	4
Value	1	10	8	15	2

↑ min

Switching index 1 and 4. Our sorted sub array now contains two elements.

Index #	0	1	2	3	4
Value	1	2	8	15	10

Pass number three we see that the minimum value, 8, is at index 2 which is the perfect position to be in the sorted sub array. Thus, we do not need to switch anything and simply place this index into the sorted sub array.

Index #	0	1	2	3	4
Value	1	2	8	15	10

With our fourth pass, we find the minimum value 10 at index 4. The end of the sorted sub array is index 2, so we want to swap index 4 with index 3.

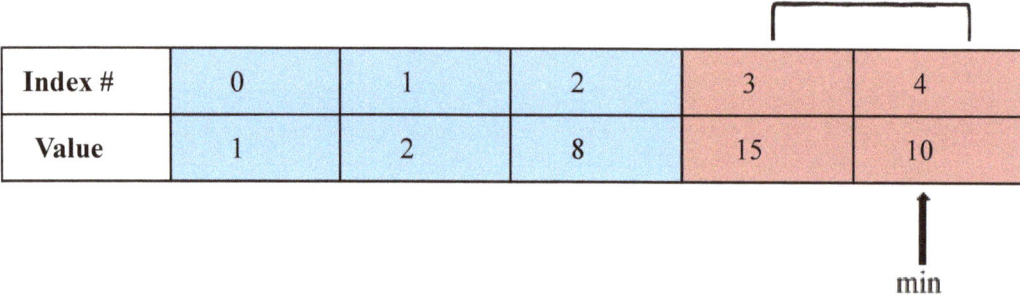

Index #	0	1	2	3	4
Value	1	2	8	15	10

The integer 10 is being entered into the sorted sub array.

Index #	0	1	2	3	4
Value	1	2	8	10	15

Obviously the last value of the array would be the largest element in the array if the previous steps were done correctly. However, an algorithm must complete all steps. So the last index will be identified as having the minimum value and inserted in the end of the sorted array, which would be at the same index, completing our sorted array.

Index #	0	1	2	3	4
Value	1	2	8	10	15

Completed sorted array:

Index #	0	1	2	3	4
Value	1	2	8	10	15

This method is incredibly ineffective with $O(n^2)$ time complexity. The larger the list, the longer it takes as the length of the array determines how many times we must pass through and check for the minimum value. Implementing the method, we can see out the before and after sorting the array will have the same output as our diagrams.

FIG 5.1: *Selection Sort*

```python
def selection_sort(arr):
    # sub array from 0 to x is sorted
    # sub array from x to len(arr) is unsorted
    for x in range(len(arr) - 1):
        # index will hold the index of the smallest element in the sub array
        index = x
        # search for the smallest element in the sub array
        for y in range(x + 1, len(arr)):
            # update index if a smaller element has been found
            if arr[y] < arr[index]:
                index = y
        # swap the smallest element so it's the last element of the sorted sub array
        smaller_number = arr[index]
        arr[index] = arr[x]
        arr[x] = smaller_number


def display_array(arr):
    for x in arr:
        print(x, end=" ")
    print()


array = [2, 10, 8, 15, 1]
print("Before sorting:", end=" ")
display_array(array)
print("After sorting:", end=" ")
selection_sort(array)
display_array(array)
```

FIG 5.2: Output after Selection Sort

```
Before sorting: 2 10 8 15 1
After sorting: 1 2 8 10 15
```

5.3 INSERTION SORT

While selection sort is obviously ineffective to humans, **insertion sort** may be a method that you have used before. This method is similar to how a person would sort a hand of cards while playing Big 2, You would move a card to place it in order as you go down your hand. Insertion sort uses a key to hold the current element that we are looking at to compare it to elements to the left to see if we need to move the location of the key. Insertion sort requires comparisons to be done between elements. Let's look at the same unsorted array with 5 integers and see how insertion sort would go about sorting it.

Index #	0	1	2	3	4
Value	2	10	8	15	1

The key will be colored blue and the element it is being compared against will be colored green. Since we need two elements in order to compare, we will set the key to be the second element of the array, so index 1.

Index #	0	1	2	3	4
Value	2	10	8	15	1

In this instance, we see that key, 10, is larger than the element to the left. Thus we do not need to move the location of the key. As a result, we will not change anything about the array, and instead move the key to the right element.

Index #	0	1	2	3	4
Value	2	10	8	15	1

The key is now at index 2 with element 8. We compare it to the element directly to the left. This time, we see that the key is less than the element to the left.and thus is not in the correct position. However, where do we know where it must be inserted? We will compare all elements left of the key until we have compared them all or found an element that is not larger than it. So now we will move from the element directly to the left of the key over one and compare the key to the element in index 0.

Index #	0	1	2	3	4
Value	2	10	8	15	1

Here the key is larger than the element it is being compared to. So we now know that the correct location to insert the key would be in front of the first element it compared to. So the key will be inserted in front of element 10.

Index #	0	1	2	3	4
Value	2	10	8	15	1

Just being clear: the two compared elements are NOT switching places. Element 8 inserted in front of element 10, causing the rest of the array to shit over to the right by 1.

Index #	0	1	2	3	4
Value	2	8	10	15	1

Now we will move the key from index 2 to index 3 and make key = 10. We compare it back to index 2. Here, we see that 15 is larger than 10 and we do not need to change any of the positions.

Index #	0	1	2	3	4
Value	2	8	10	15	1

Now we will move the key to the final element which is index 4. First comparing it to the element directly to the left of it. We see that the key is smaller and needs to be relocated.

Index #	0	1	2	3	4
Value	2	8	10	15	1

Once again we need to find the new location. Moving one over to the left we compare 10 and 1.

Index #	0	1	2	3	4
Value	2	8	10	15	1

Key is smaller than 10, we move over to the left once again.

Index #	0	1	2	3	4
Value	2	8	10	15	1

Key is smaller than 8, we move over to the left.

Index #	0	1	2	3	4
Value	2	8	10	15	1

Key is smaller than 2, but there is no element to the left of 2. We are out of bounds and back to the front of the array. Thus, we know that we must insert the key at the front of the array.

Index #	0	1	2	3	4
Value	2	8	10	15	1

We insert the key to the front and shift the rest of the elements in the array. Since the key was at the end of the array, we have sorted the entire array using insertion sort.

Index #	0	1	2	3	4
Value	1	2	8	10	15

Now, let's see the implementation of this method.

FIG 5.3: Insertion Sort

```python
def insertion_sort(arr):
    # traverses the array
    for x in range(1, len(arr)):
        # key stores the current element, which is to be sorted into its correct position
        # check elements on its left to find its correct place in the array
        key = arr[x]
        # y stores the indexes of the elements on the left key
        y = x - 1
        # while y is in bounds and key is less than arr[y] (an element on key's left)
        while y >= 0 and key < arr[y]:
            # shift the array down one position
            arr[y + 1] = arr[y]
            # decrease the value of y to continue checking the elements on the left key to find key's correct place
            y -= 1
        # place key in its correct position
        arr[y + 1] = key


def display_array(arr):
    for x in arr:
        print(x, end=" ")
    print()
```

```
25    array = [2, 10, 8, 15, 1]
26    print("Before sorting:", end=" ")
27    display_array(array)
28    print("After sorting:", end=" ")
29    insertion_sort(array)
30    display_array(array)
```

FIG 5.4: Output of insertion sort

```
Before sorting: 2 10 8 15 1
After sorting: 1 2 8 10 15
```

5.4 BUBBLE SORT

Bubble sorting is a simple sorting method, although it is not always the most efficient. When using bubble sort to organize a set of elements, you compare each element to the element adjacent to it. When necessary, you swap the two elements to follow the order you have chosen. For example, if you are sorting the set in ascending order, you would swap the two elements so that the element with the bigger value comes after the element with the smaller value. Then, you repeat this process of comparing and swapping when necessary until the set is properly organized.

In the following example, we will be sorting an array so that it is organized from least to greatest. Here is our array:

Index #	0	1	2	3	4
Value	2	10	8	15	1

Each round of bubble sorting will go through the entire array once. At the end of each round, you will know that at least one element is in the correct place. Thus, the number of rounds it takes to bubble sort corresponds to the size of the array. In this example, the array has 5 elements. Therefore, we need to complete 5 rounds of bubble sorting.

Round 1

Step 1: Compare the value at index 0 to the value at index 1. 2 is less than 10, so these values do not swap.

Index #	0	1	2	3	4
Value	2	10	8	15	1

Step 2: Compare the value at index 1 to the value at index 2. 10 is greater than 8, so these values swap.

Index #	0	1	2	3	4
Value	2	10	8	15	1

Swap the value at index 1 with the value at index 2.

Index #	0	1	2	3	4
Value	2	8	10	15	1

Step 3: Compare the value at index 2 to the value at index 3. 10 is less than 15, so these values do not swap.

Index #	0	1	2	3	4
Value	2	8	10	15	1

Step 4: Compare the value at index 3 to that at index 4. 15 is greater than 1, so these values swap.

Index #	0	1	2	3	4
Value	2	8	10	15	1

Swap the value at index 3 with the value at index 4.

Index #	0	1	2	3	4
Value	2	8	10	1	5

This completes the first round of bubble sorting. With one round down, we have established that the last element in the array is now in the correct place.

Round 2

Step 1: Compare the value at index 0 to that at index 1. 2 is less than 8, so these values do not swap.

Index #	0	1	2	3	4
Value	2	8	10	1	15

Notice that even though you know these values are in the proper order from looking at it, it is crucial to perform this step to check. The computer cannot immediately recognize that an array is sorted in the way that humans can.

Step 2: Compare the value at index 1 to that at index 2. 8 is less than 10, so these values do not swap.

Index #	0	1	2	3	4
Value	2	8	10	1	15

Step 3: Compare the value at index 2 to that at index 3. 10 is greater than 1, so these values swap.

Index #	0	1	2	3	4
Value	2	8	10	1	15

Swap the value at index 2 with the value at index 3.

Index #	0	1	2	3	4
Value	2	8	1	10	15

Step 4: Compare the value at index 3 to that at index 4. 10 is less than 15, so these values do not swap.

Index #	0	1	2	3	4
Value	2	8	1	10	15

This completes the second round of bubble sorting. With two rounds down, we have established that the last two elements in the array are now in the correct place.

Round 3

Step 1: Compare the value at index 0 to that at index 1. 2 is less than 8, so these values do not swap.

Index #	0	1	2	3	4
Value	2	8	1	10	15

Step 2: Compare the value at index 1 to that at index 2. 8 is greater than 1, so these values swap.

Index #	0	1	2	3	4
Value	2	8	1	10	15

Swap the value at index 1 with the value at index 2.

Index #	0	1	2	3	4
Value	2	1	8	10	15

Step 3: Compare the value at index 2 to that at index 3. 8 is less than 10, so these values do not swap.

Index #	0	1	2	3	4
Value	2	1	8	10	15

Step 4: Compare the value at index 3 to that at index 4. 10 is less than 15, so these values do not swap.

Index #	0	1	2	3	4
Value	2	1	8	10	15

This completes the third round of bubble sorting. With three rounds down, we have established that the last three elements in the array are now in the correct place.

Round 4

Step 1: Compare the value at index 0 to that at index 1. 2 is greater than 1, so these values swap.

Index #	0	1	2	3	4
Value	2	1	8	10	15

Swap the values at index 0 with the value at index 1.

Index #	0	1	2	3	4
Value	1	2	8	10	15

Step 2: Compare the value at index 1 to that at index 2. 2 is less than 8, so these values do not swap.

Index #	0	1	2	3	4
Value	1	2	8	10	15

Step 3: Compare the value at index 2 to that at index 3. 8 is less than 10, so these values do not swap.

Index #	0	1	2	3	4
Value	1	2	8	10	15

Step 4: Compare the value at index 3 to that at index 4. 10 is less than 15, so these values do not swap.

Index #	0	1	2	3	4
Value	1	2	8	10	15

This completes the fourth round of bubble sorting. With four rounds down, we have established that the last four elements in the array are now in the correct place.

Round 5

Even though we know the array is sorted, the basic bubble sort algorithm will still execute round 5.

Step 1: Compare the value at index 0 to that at index 1. 1 is less than 2, so these values do not swap.

Index #	0	1	2	3	4
Value	1	2	8	10	15

Step 2: Compare the value at index 1 to that at index 2. 2 is less than 8, so these values do not swap.

Index #	0	1	2	3	4
Value	1	2	8	10	15

Step 3: Compare the value at index 2 to that at index 3. 8 is less than 10, so these values do not swap.

Index #	0	1	2	3	4
Value	1	2	8	10	15

Step 4: Compare the value at index 3 to that at index 4. 10 is less than 15, so these values do not swap.

Index #	0	1	2	3	4
Value	2	1	8	10	15

This step completes the fifth round of bubble sorting. With five rounds down, we have established that the last five elements in the array are now in the correct place. All of the elements in the array are in the right place, so we are done sorting.

To apply the concept of bubble sorting to programming, the code might look like the following:

FIG 5.5: Bubble Sort

```python
def bubble_sort(arr):
    # for every element in the array
    for x in range(len(arr)):
        # for every element in the array while in bounds
        for y in range(len(arr) - 1):
            # if the value on the right is less than the current element
            if arr[y] > arr[y + 1]:
                # swap
                temp = arr[y]
                arr[y] = arr[y + 1]
                arr[y + 1] = temp


def display_array(arr):
    for x in arr:
        print(x, end=" ")
    print()


array = [2, 10, 8, 15, 1]
print("Before sorting:", end=" ")
display_array(array)
print("After sorting:", end=" ")
bubble_sort(array)
display_array(array)
```

FIG 5.6: *Output of Bubble Sort*

```
Before sorting: 2 10 8 15 1
After sorting: 1 2 8 10 15
```

5.5 QUICK SORT

Quick sort is a common sorting algorithm that uses a divide-and-conquer approach, meaning it divides a large problem into smaller problems and finds a solution recursively. Eventually, by solving the sub-problems, the algorithm is able to solve the larger problem.

Quick sort is often more efficient than bubble sort, but it has a much higher complexity because it is a recursive algorithm. Quick sort's best case runtime is $O(n \log n)$ and its worst case runtime is $O(n^2)$. Quick sort is advantageous because it is an in-place sorting algorithm, so it sorts in place and requires no extra memory. Other sorting algorithms such as merge sort require additional memory in the form of temporary arrays.

Quick sort is unique because it utilizes a pivot element, and this element is significant because it determines the runtime of the algorithm. The pivot element can be at any position in the sorting set. It can be the first element, the last element, or somewhere in the middle. Quick sort also utilizes partitioning, or the dividing of the sorting set into smaller sets.

In this chapter, we will use an array to demonstrate quick sort. The general procedure for quick sort is as follows:

1. Pick a pivot element of the array. In our implementation, we will choose the element in the middle of the array.
2. While lowerIndex is less than or equal to upperIndex, we do the following:
    a. While the value of the array at lowerIndex (arr[lowerIndex]) is less than the pivot, increment lowerIndex. Once arr[lowerIndex] is greater than or equal to pivot, stop incrementing lowerIndex.
    b. While the value of the array at upperIndex (arr[upperIndex]) is greater than pivot, decrement upperIndex. Once arr[upperIndex] is less than or equal to pivot, stop decrementing upperIndex.
    c. If lowerIndex is less than or equal to upperIndex, swap the values of the array at lowerIndex and upperIndex, increment

lowerIndex, and decrement upperIndex. In other words, arr[lowerIndex] will equal the value at arr[upperIndex], and arr[upperIndex] will equal the value at arr[lowerIndex].
3. If lowerBound is less than upperIndex, we use steps 1-4 on a subarray of our array.
4. If lowerIndex is less than upperBound, we use steps 1-4 on a subarray of our array.

Let's try an example. Here's our array:

Index #	0	1	2	3	4	5	6
Value	9	3	2	6	7	5	1

The following diagram is an overview of how quick sort works for our array. Refer back to this diagram as you read through the explanation for quick sort.

FIG 5.7: Overview of quick sort

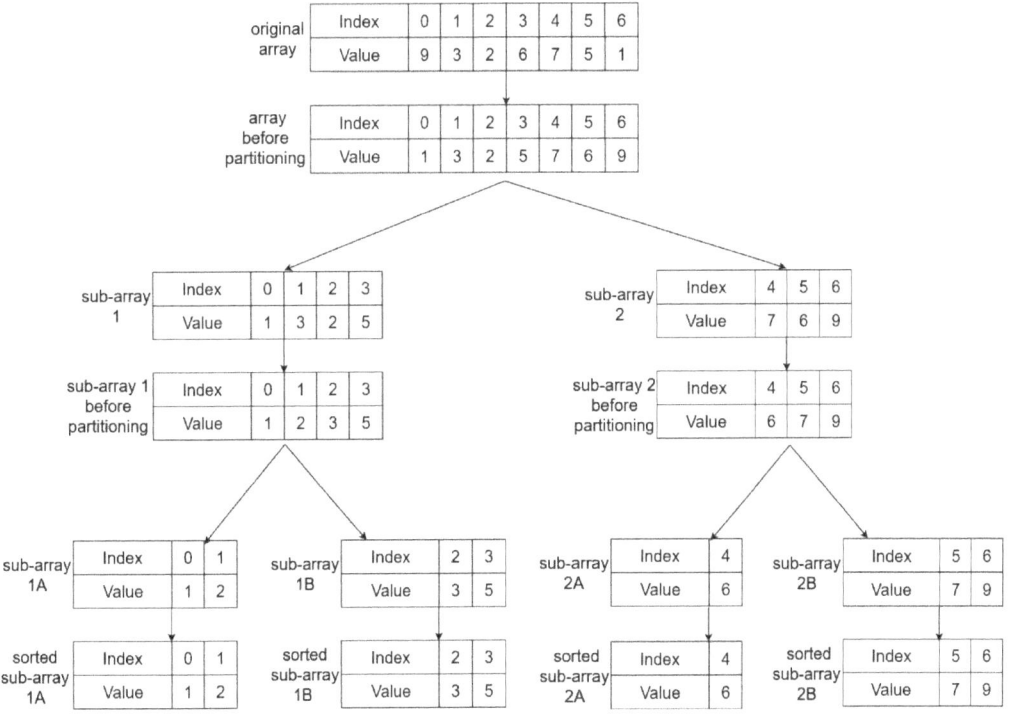

Step 1: The first step is choosing a pivot element. In this example, our pivot will be in the middle of the array. Our pivot is the value at index 3 indicated in green: 6.

Index #	0	1	2	3	4	5	6
Value	9	3	2	6	7	5	1

Step 2: The bounds of our sorting set are indicated by 2 variables called lowerBound and upperBound. The lowerBound variable is the index we want to begin sorting at, and the upperBound variable is the index we want to stop sorting at. Because we are sorting our entire array, the lowerBound is equal to 0 and the upperBound is equal to 6. To implement quick sort, we need 2 variables called lowerIndex and upperIndex. The lowerIndex variable is set to lowerBound, or 0, and the upperIndex variable is set to upperBound, or 6. While lowerIndex is less than or equal to upperIndex, we do the following:

A. While the value of the array at lowerIndex (arr[lowerIndex]) is less than pivot, increment lowerIndex. Once arr[lowerIndex] is greater than or equal to pivot, stop incrementing lowerIndex.

The lowerIndex variable (indicated in red) begins at 0, and the upperIndex variable (indicated in blue) begins at 6. Pivot equals 6. Because arr[lowerIndex] is 9 and therefore greater than pivot, we do not increment lowerIndex. The lowerIndex variable remains 0.

Index #	0	1	2	3	4	5	6
Value	9	3	2	6	7	5	1

B. While the value of the array at upperIndex (arr[upperIndex]) is greater than pivot, decrement upperIndex. Once arr[upperIndex] is less than or equal to pivot, stop decrementing upperIndex.

Because arr[upperIndex] is 1 and therefore less than pivot, we do not decrement upperIndex. The upperIndex variable remains 6.

Index #	0	1	2	3	4	5	6
Value	9	3	2	6	7	5	1

C. If lowerIndex is less than or equal to upperIndex, swap the values of the array at lowerIndex and upperIndex, increment lowerIndex, and decrement upperIndex. In other words, arr[lowerIndex] will equal the value at arr[upperIndex], and arr[upperIndex] will equal the value at arr[lowerIndex].

We swap the values of the array at arr[lowerIndex] and arr[upperIndex] because lowerIndex is less than upperIndex.

Index #	0	1	2	3	4	5	6
Value	1	3	2	6	7	5	9

We increment lowerIndex and decrement upperIndex.

Index #	0	1	2	3	4	5	6
Value	1	3	2	6	7	5	9

Now, we repeat steps A, B, C, until the loweIndex variable is greater than upperIndex and the while loop stops.

A. While the value of the array at lowerIndex 9arr[lowerIndex]) is less than pivot, increment lowerIndex. Once arr[lowerIndex] is greater than or equal to pivot, stop incrementing lowerIndex.

Because arr[lowerIndex] is 3 and therefore less than pivot, we increment lowerIndex. The lowerIndex variable becomes 2.

Index #	0	1	2	3	4	5	6
Value	1	3	2	6	7	5	9

Because arr[lowerIndex] is 2 and therefore less than pivot, we increment lowerIndex. The lowerIndex variable becomes 3.

Index #	0	1	2	3	4	5	6
Value	1	3	2	6	7	5	9

Because arr[lowerIndex] is 6 and therefore equal to pivot, we do not increment lowerIndex. The lowerIndex variable remains 3.

Index #	0	1	2	3	4	5	6
Value	1	3	2	6	7	5	9

B. While the value of the array at upperIndex (arr[upperIndex]) is greater than pivot, decrement upperIndex. Once arr[upperIndex] is less than or equal to pivot, stop decrementing upperIndex.

Because arr[upperIndex] is 5 and therefore less than pivot, we do not decrement upperIndex. The upperIndex variable remains 5.

Index #	0	1	2	3	4	5	6
Value	1	3	2	6	7	5	9

C. If lowerIndex is less than or equal to upperIndex, swap the values of the array at lowerIndex and upperIndex, increment lowerIndex, and decrement upperIndex. In other words, arr[lowerIndex] will equal the value at arr[upperIndex], and arr[upperIndex] will equal the value at arr[lowerIndex].

We swap the values of the array at arr[lowerIndex] and arr[upperIndex] because lowerIndex is less than upperIndex.

Index #	0	1	2	3	4	5	6
Value	1	3	2	5	7	6	9

We increment lowerIndex and decrement upperIndex. The purple shading indicates that lowerIndex and upperIndex are the same value.

Index #	0	1	2	3	4	5	6
Value	1	3	2	5	7	6	9

Because lowerIndex is still less than or equal to upperIndex, we repeat the previous steps.

A. While the value of the array at lowerIndex (arr[lowerIndex]) is less than pivot, increment lowerIndex. Once arr[lowerIndex] is greater than or equal to pivot, stop incrementing lowerIndex.

Because arr[lowerIndex] is 7 and therefore greater than pivot, we do not increment lowerIndex. The lowerIndex variable remains 4.

Index #	0	1	2	3	4	5	6
Value	1	3	2	5	7	6	9

Because lowerIndex is greater than upperIndex, the while loop of Step 2 stops.

Step 3: Remember, lowerBound and upperBound indicate the bounds of our sorting set. If lowerBound is less than upperIndex, we use quick sort on a sub-array of our array. This is sub-array 1 in figure 4.3. The sub-array has the same lowerBound as the array it's inside of, but its upperBound is set to the upperIndex of the array it's inside of. Therefore, the sub-array begins at index 0 and ends at index 3. Here is our sub-array:

Index #	0	1	2	3
Value	1	3	2	5

To perform quick sort on this sub-array, we must follow steps 1-4.

1) The first step is choosing a pivot element. The pivot is in the middle of the array. In this case, the middle is between index 1 and 2. we'll round down to 1. Our pivot is the value at index 1 indicated by green: 3.

Index #	0	1	2	3
Value	1	3	2	5

2) While lowerIndex is less than or equal to upperIndex, we do the following:

a. While the value of the array at lowerIndex (arr[lowerIndex]) is less than pivot, increment lowerIndex. Once arr[lowerIndex] is greater than or equal to pivot, stop incrementing lowerIndex.

Because arr[lowerIndex] is 1 and therefore less than pivot, we increment lowerIndex. The lowerIndex variable becomes 1.

Index #	0	1	2	3
Value	1	3	2	5

Because arr[lowerIndex] is 3 and therefore equal to pivot, we do not increment lowerIndex. The lowerIndex variable remains 1.

Index #	0	1	2	3
Value	1	3	2	5

b. While the value of the array at upperIndex (arr[upperIndex]) is greater than pivot, decrement upperIndex. Once arr[upperIndex] is less than or equal to pivot, stop decrementing upperIndex.

Because arr[upperIndex] is 5 and therefore greater than pivot, we decrement upperIndex. The upperIndex variable becomes 2.

Index #	0	1	2	3
Value	1	3	2	5

Because arr[upperIndex] is 2 and therefore less than pivot, we do not decrement upperIndex. The upperIndex variable remains 2.

Index #	0	1	2	3
Value	1	3	2	5

c. If lowerIndex is less than or equal to upperIndex, swap the values of the array at lowerIndex and upperIndex, increment lowerIndex, and decrement upperIndex. In other words, arr[lowerIndex] will equal the value at arr[upperIndex], and arr[upperIndex] will equal the value at arr[lowerIndex].

We swap the values of the array at arr[lowerIndex] and arr[upperIndex] because lowerIndex is less than upperIndex.

Index #	0	1	2	3
Value	1	2	3	5

We increment lowerIndex and decrement upperIndex.

Index #	0	1	2	3
Value	1	2	3	5

Because lowerIndex is greater than upperIndex, the while loop of Step 2 stops.

3) If lowerBound is less than upperIndex, we use quick sort on a subarray of our sub-array. This is sub-array 1A in figure 4.3. The subarray has the same

lowerBound as the array it's inside of, but its upperBound is set to upperIndex of the array it's inside of. Therefore, the sub-array begins at index 0 and ends at index 1. Here is our sub-array:

Index #	0	1
Value	1	2

To perform quick sort on this sub-array, we must follow steps 1-4.

1) The first step is choosing a pivot element. The pivot is in the middle of the array. In this case, the middle is between index 0 and 1. We'll round down to 0. Our pivot is the value at index 0 indicated in green: 1.

Index #	0	1
Value	1	2

2) While lowerIndex is less than or equal to upperIndex, we do the following:

a. While the value of the array at lowerIndex (arr[lowerIndex]) is less than pivot, increment lowerIndex. Once arr[lowerIndex] is greater than or equal to pivot, stop incrementing lowerIndex.

Because arr[lowerIndex] is 1 and therefore equal to pivot, we do not increment lowerIndex. The lowerIndex variable remains 0.

Index #	0	1
Value	1	2

b. While the value of the array at upperIndex (arr[upperIndex]) is greater than pivot, decrement upperIndex. Once arr[upperIndex] is less than or equal to pivot, stop decrementing upperIndex.

Because arr[upperIndex] is 2 and therefore greater than pivot, we decrement upperIndex. The upperIndex variable becomes 0.

Index #	0	1
Value	1	2

Because ar[upperIndex] is 1 and therefore equal to pivot, we do not decrement upperIndex. The upperIndex variable remains 0.

Index #	0	1
Value	1	2

c. If lowerIndex is less than or equal to upperIndex, swap the values of the array at lowerIndex and upperIndex, increment lowerIndex, and decrement upperIndex. In other words, arr[lowerIndex] will equal the value at arr[upperIndex], and are[upperIndex] will equal the value at arr[lowerIndex].

We swap the values of the array at a[lowerIndex] and arr[upperIndex] because lowerIndex is equal to upperIndex.

Index #	0	1
Value	1	2

We increment lowerIndex and decrement upperIndex.

Index #	0	1
Value	1	2

Because lowerIndex is greater than upperIndex, the while loop of Step 2 stops.

3) If lowerBound is less than upperIndex, we use quick sort on a sub-array of our sub-array. We do not do this because lowerBound equals 0 and upperIndex equals -1.

4) If lowerIndex is less than upperBound, we use quick sort on a sub-array of our sub-array. We do not do this because lowerIndex equals 1 and upperBound equals 1.

If lowerIndex is less than upperBound, we use quick sort on a subarray of our sub-array. This is sub-array 1B in figure 4.3. The subarray has the same upperBound as the array it's inside of, but its lowerBound is set to the lowerIndex of the array it's inside of. Therefore, the sub-array begins at index 2 and ends at index 3. Here is our sub-array:

Index #	2	3
Value	3	5

To perform quick sort on this sub-array, we must follow steps 1-4.

1) The first step is choosing a pivot element. The pivot is in the middle of the array. In this case, the middle is between index 2 and 3. We'll round down to 2. Our pivot is the value at index 2 indicated in green: 3.

Index #	2	3
Value	3	5

2) While lowerIndex is less than or equal to upperIndex, we do the following:
a. While the value of the array at lowerIndex (arr[lowerIndex]) is less than pivot, increment lowerIndex. Once arr[lowerIndex] is greater than or equal to pivot, stop incrementing lowerIndex.

Because arr[lowerIndex] is 3 and therefore equal to pivot, we do not increment lowerIndex. The lowerIndex variable remains 2.

Index #	2	3
Value	3	5

b. While the value of the array at upperIndex (arr[upperIndex]) is greater than pivot, decrement upperIndex. Once arr[upperIndex] is less than or equal to pivot, stop decrementing upperIndex.

Because arr[upperIndex] is 5 and therefore greater than pivot, we decrement upperIndex. The upperIndex variable becomes 2.

Index #	2	3
Value	3	5

Because arr[upperIndex] is 3 and therefore equal to pivot, we do not decrement upperIndex. The upperIndex variable remains 2.

Index #	2	3
Value	3	5

c. If lowerIndex is less than or equal to upperIndex, swap the values of the array at lowerIndex and upperIndex, increment lowerIndex, and decrement upperIndex. In other words, arr[lowerIndex] will equal the value at arr[upperIndex], and arr[upperIndex] will equal the value at arr[lowerIndex].

We swap the values of the array at arr[lowerIndex] and arr[upperIndex] because lowerIndex is equal to upperIndex.

Index #	2	3
Value	3	5

We increment lowerIndex and decrement upperIndex.

Index #	2	3
Value	3	5

Because lowerIndex is greater than upperIndex, the while loop of Step 2 stops.

3) If lowerBound is less than upperIndex, we use quick sort on a sub-array of our sub-array. Since lowerBound equals 2 and upperIndex equals 1, we do not change.

4) If lowerIndex is less than upperBound, we use quick sort on a sub-array of our sub-array. Since lowerIndex equals 3 and upperBound equals 3, we do not change.

Step 4: If lowerIndex is less than upperBound, we use quick sort on a sub-array of our array. This is sub-array 2 in figure 4.3. The sub-array has the same upperBound as the array it's inside of, but its lowerBound is set to lowerIndex of the array it's inside of. Therefore, the sub-array begins at index 4 and ends at index 6. Here is our sub-array:

Index #	4	5	6
Value	7	6	9

To perform quick sort on this sub-array, we must follow steps 1-4.

1) The first step is choosing a pivot element. The pivot is in the middle of the array. In this case, the middle is at index 5. Our pivot is the value at index 5 indicated in green: 6.

Index #	4	5	6
Value	7	6	9

2) While lowerIndex is less than or equal to upperIndex, we do the following:

a. While the value of the array at lowerIndex (arr[lowerIndex]) is less than pivot, increment lowerIndex. Once arr[lowerIndex] is greater than or equal to pivot, stop incrementing lowerIndex.

Because arr[lowerIndex] is 7 and therefore greater than pivot, we do not increment lowerIndex. The lowerIndex variable remains 4.

Index #	4	5	6
Value	7	6	9

b. While the value of the array at upperIndex (arr[upperIndex]) is greater than pivot, decrement upperIndex. Once arr[upperIndex] is less than or equal to pivot, stop decrementing upperIndex.

Because arr[upperIndex] is 9 and therefore greater than pivot, we decrement upperIndex. The upperIndex variable becomes 5.

Index #	4	5	6
Value	7	6	9

Because arr[upperIndex] is 6 and therefore equal to pivot, we do not decrement upperIndex. The upperIndex variable remains 5.

Index #	4	5	6
Value	7	6	9

c. If lowerIndex is less than or equal to upperIndex, swap the values of the array at lowerIndex and upperIndex, increment lowerIndex, and decrement upperIndex. In other words, arr[lowerIndex] will equal the value at arr[upperIndex], and arr[upperIndex] will equal the value at arr[lowerIndex].

We swap the values of the array at arr[lowerIndex] and arr[upperIndex] because lowerIndex is less than upperIndex.

Index #	4	5	6
Value	6	7	9

We increment lowerIndex and decrement upperIndex.

Index #	4	5	6
Value	6	7	9

Because lowerIndex is greater than upperIndex, the while loop of Step 2 stops.

3) If lowerBound is less than upperIndex, we use quick sort on a subarray of our sub-array. We do not do this because lowerBound equals 4 and upperIndex equals 4. Therefore, the sub-array 2A in figure 4.3 does not technically get created.

4) If lowerIndex is less than upperBound, we use quick sort on a subarray of our sub-array. This is sub-array 2B in figure 4.3. The subarray has the same upperBound as the array it's inside of, but its lowerBound is set to lowerIndex of the array it's inside of.

Therefore, the sub-array begins at index 5 and ends at index 6. Here is our sub-array:

Index #	5	6
Value	7	9

To perform quick sort on this sub-array, we must follow steps 1-4.

1) The first step is choosing a pivot element. The pivot is in the middle of the array. In this case, the middle is between index 5 and 6. We'll round down to 5. Our pivot is the value at index 5 indicated in green: 7.

Index #	5	6

Value	7	9

2) While lowerIndex is less than or equal to upperIndex, we do the following:

a) While the value of the array at lowerIndex (arr[lowerIndex]) is less than pivot, increment lowerIndex. Once arr[lowerIndex] is greater than or equal to pivot, stop incrementing lowerIndex.

Because arr[lowerIndex] is 7 and therefore equal to pivot, we do not increment lowerIndex. The lowerIndex variable remains 5.

Index #	5	6
Value	7	9

b) While the value of the array at upperIndex (arr[upperIndex]) is greater than pivot, decrement upperIndex. Once arr[upperIndex] is less than or equal to pivot, stop decrementing upperIndex.

Because arr[upperIndex] is 9 and therefore greater than pivot, we decrement upperIndex. The upperIndex variable becomes 5.

Index #	5	6
Value	7	9

Because arr[upperIndex] is 7 and therefore equal to pivot, we do not decrement upperIndex. The upperIndex variable remains 5.

Index #	5	6
Value	7	9

c) If lowerIndex is less than or equal to upperIndex, swap the values of the array at lowerIndex and upperIndex, increment lowerIndex, and decrement upperIndex. In other words, arr[lowerIndex] will equal the value at arr[upperIndex], and arr[upperIndex] will equal the value at arr[lowerIndex].

We swap the values of the array at arr[lowerIndex] and arr[upperIndex] because lowerIndex is equal to upperIndex.

Index #	5	6
Value	7	9

We increment lowerIndex and decrement upperIndex.

Index #	5	6
Value	7	9

Because lowerIndex is greater than upperIndex, the while loop of Step 2 stops.

3) If lowerBound is less than upperIndex, we use quick sort on a sub-array of our sub-array. Since lowerBound equals 5 and upperIndex equals 4, we do not change.

4) If lowerIndex is less than upperBound, we use quick sort on a sub-array of our sub-array. Since lowerIndex equals 6 and upperBound equals 6, we do not change.

We are finished using quick sort to sort our array! Our array now looks like this:

Index #	0	1	2	3	4	5	6
Value	1	2	3	5	6	7	9

An implementation of quick sort might look like the following:

FIG 5.8: Quick Sort

```python
def quick_sort(arr, lower_bound, upper_bound):
    # pick the pivot element (middle element in this case)
    pivot = arr[lower_bound + int((upper_bound - lower_bound) / 2)]
    # variables initially equal to lower and upper bounds, but change as array is traversed
    lower_index = lower_bound
    upper_index = upper_bound
    # traverse array so indexes approach each other
    # once they overlap, loop stops
    while lower_index <= upper_index:
        # start on the left of pivot and find the first element greater than pivot
        while arr[lower_index] < pivot:
            lower_index += 1
        # start on the right of pivot and find the first element less than pivot
        while arr[upper_index] > pivot:
            upper_index -= 1
        # all elements less than pivot on its left and all elements greater than pivot on its right
        # only swap elements if upper and lower indexes haven't overlapped
        if lower_index <= upper_index:
```

```python
                # swap lower and upper index element
                temp = arr[lower_index]
                arr[lower_index] = arr[upper_index]
                arr[upper_index] = temp
                # change values of lower and upper index to continue traversing the array
                # so indexes are approaching each other
                lower_index += 1
                upper_index -= 1
        # pivot is in final place
        # if lower_bound is less than upper_index
        # recursively call quick_sort on sub array between lower_bound and upper_index
        if lower_bound < upper_index:
            quick_sort(arr, lower_bound, upper_index)
        # if lower index is less than upper bound
        # recursively call quick_sort on sub array between lower_index and upper_bound
        # if not, stop because base case is reached
        if lower_index < upper_bound:
            quick_sort(arr, lower_index, upper_bound)


def display_array(arr):
    for x in arr:
        print(x, end=" ")
    print()


array = [9, 3, 2, 6, 7, 5, 1]
print("Before sorting:", end=" ")
display_array(array)
print("After sorting:", end=" ")
quick_sort(array, 0, len(array) - 1)
display_array(array)
```

FIG 5.9: Output of Quick Sort

```
Before sorting: 9 3 2 6 7 5 1
After sorting: 1 2 3 5 6 7 9
```

5.6 MERGE SORT

Merge sort works by recursively dividing an array into smaller sub arrays, sorting the small sub arrays, and then merging them back into the large sub array. It divides an array of *n* elements into *n* sub arrays by recursively splitting each sub array in half until the sub arrays only contain one element. Then, it merges these sub arrays together so that they are sorted, and we end up with one array, which is the sorted array.

Let's examine an example of this unsorted array.

Index #	0	1	2	3	4	5
Value	6	5	14	2	8	7

Here we have an array and the first thing we want to do is divide it into two arrays. We do so by creating two variables called start and end. The start is the beginning of the array which is 0 and the end is the last index which is 5. We must check that start is less than end, which 0 is less than 5. Since the start is less than 5, we are allowed to split. The middle of the array is the formula **(start + end)/2**. In this case, (0+5)/2 = 2.5. That means the middle is in between index 2 and index 3. We will round down and say that the middle is at index 2 and this is where we will cleave the array. We will create two arrays, Sub Array 1. will go from index 0 to 2 and Sub Array 1 goes from index 3 to 5.

Sub Array 1

0	1	2
6	5	14

Sub Array 2

3	4	5
2	8	7

We will be following the Sub Array 1 first as the MergeSort method is continued to be called on it. Once again we assign the start and end values. Start, 0, is less than end, 2, so we are going to divide the array. The middle of the array is at index 1. So we are creating two more arrays with Sub Array 1.1 going from index 0 to 1 and Sub Array 1.2 just being index 2.

Sub Array 1.1

0	1
6	5

Sub Array 1.2

2
14

Now we call MargeSort once again upon both of these arrays. For Sub Array 1.1, start is equal to 0 and end is equal to 1. Start is lower than end so we will cleave the array. The center is 0.5, in between the arrays. So we round down and create one array containing index 0 and one containing index 1. For Array 1.2, start is equal to 2 and end is equal to 2. Since start is not less than end, as 2 is not less than 2, we will not cleave sub array 1.2 (as we cannot leave one element).

Sub Array 1.1.1

0
6

Sub Array 1.1.2

1
5

Sub Array 1.2

2
14

We are unable to further divide any of these arrays. The start and end values of each of these arrays are equal to each other and thus will not allow the computer to cleave the arrays, Now it is time to merge. We are going to merge these broken arrays into a temporary array. So first, Sub Array 1.1.1 and 1.1.2 will be sorted into a temporary array. Since the data of Sub Array 1.1.2 is larger than 1.1.1, it will be added first to the temporary array. Merging the two together, we have begun building up an array.

Temp Array 1

0	1
5	6

Sub Array 1.2

2
14

Now Sub Array 1.2 will be added to our temporary array.

Tempo Array 1

0	1	2
6	5	14

With this temporary array completed, when the method MergeSort is used, we recursively return back to the original array and look at the two sub arrays. Sub Array 1 has been sorted, but now we must sort Sub Array 2. Doing the process all over, we set start to 3 and end to 5. 3 is smaller than 5, so we find the middle to be about 4 and create two sub arrays.

Sub Array 2.1

3	4
2	8

Sub Array 2.2

5
7

We call the method MergeSort again. For Sub Array 2.1, start is equal to 3 and end is equal to 4. The middle is rounded down to 3 and we cleave the sub array. For Sub Array 2.2, we do not need to cleave it as start is not less than end.

Sub Array 2.1.1

3
2

Sub Array 2.1.2

4
8

Sub Array 2.2

5
7

With the arrays now only containing one element and not being able to be broken down further as the start is not less than the end of each of the sub arrays, we will begin merging again. A temporary array is made that merges 2.1.1 and 2.1.2 sorted.

Temp Array 2

3	4
2	8

Sub Array 2.2

5
7

Now Sub Array 2.2 is merged into our temporary array while being sorted. The element 7 must be inserted after element 3 in the temporary array.

Tempo Array 2

3	4	5
2	8	7

At last, we have two merged temporary arrays. The last thing that must be completed is merging the two arrays together and sorted as it is merged.

Temp Array 1

0	1	2
6	5	14

Temp Array 2

3	4	5
2	8	7

Merged Array is now sorted.

Index #	0	1	2	3	4	5
Value	2	5	6	7	8	14

We had followed through the process as it occurred. The following diagram makes it appear that some processes occur simultaneously while they do not; however, it better helps understand how the array is being divided and merged in this process.

FIG 5.10: *Overview of Merge Sort*

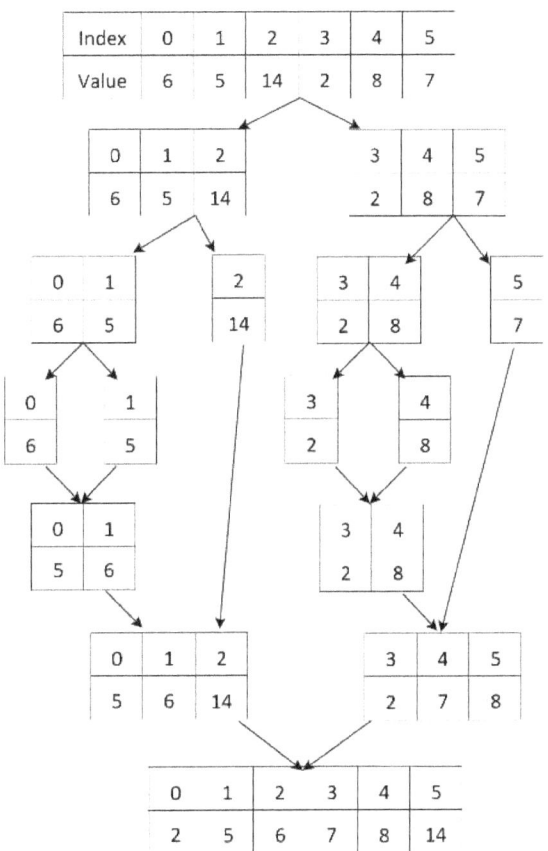

Now we will implement merge sort.

FIG 5.11: *Merge Sort*

```python
def merge_sort(arr, left, right):
    # if there is more than one element in the sub array
    if left < right:
        # calculate middle index to split array in half
        mid = int((left + right) / 2)
        # call merge_sort on first half of array
        merge_sort(arr, left, mid)
        # call merge_sort on second half of array
        merge_sort(arr, mid + 1, right)
        # call merge on two sub arrays
        merge(arr, left, mid, right)


# method that merges two sub arrays from indexes left to mid and mid + 1 to right
def merge(arr, left, mid, right):
    # temporary array to hold merged sub arrays
    temp = [None] * (right - left + 1)
    # index x to traverse first sub array
    x = left
    # index y to traverse second sub array
    y = mid + 1
    # index used to traverse temporary array
    z = 0
    # traverse both arrays and in each iteration add smaller of both elements in temp
    while x <= mid and y <= right:
        if arr[x] <= arr[y]:
            temp[z] = arr[x]
            z += 1
            x += 1
        else:
            temp[z] = arr[y]
            z += 1
            y += 1
```

```python
        # add elements left in the first sub array
        while x <= mid:
            temp[z] = arr[x]
            z += 1
            x += 1
        # add elements left in the second sub array
        while y <= right:
            temp[z] = arr[y]
            z += 1
            y += 1
        # copy temp to original array
        for i in range(left, right + 1):
            arr[i] = temp[i - left]


def display_array(arr):
    for x in arr:
        print(x, end=" ")
    print()


array = [6, 5, 14, 2, 8, 7]
print("Before sorting:", end=" ")
display_array(array)
print("After sorting:", end=" ")
merge_sort(array, 0, len(array) - 1)
display_array(array)
```

FIG 5.12: Output of Merge Sort

```
Before sorting: 6 5 14 2 8 7
After sorting: 2 5 6 7 8 14
```

Chapter 6 Searching

CHAPTER CONTENTS

6.1 Introduction: Searching
6.2 Big O Notation
6.3 Linear Search
6.4 Binary Search
6.5 Depth First Search
6.6 Breadth First Search

6.1 INTRODUCTION: SEARCHING

When multiple pieces of information are stored or organized together in a data structure, you might encounter a situation in which you need to find a specific piece of information. Various searching methods have been created for the purposes of searching data structures. In this chapter, we will focus on the logic behind **linear** and **binary search** methods.

6.2 BIG O NOTATION

When describing the efficiency of different searching algorithms, programmers use a mathematical notation called **Big O**. Big O notation refers to the **time-complexity** of the algorithm. This notation explains how quickly the **runtime** of the algorithm grows as the data structure gets bigger. In simpler terms, Big O notation can be used to describe how the increase in the size of the data set affects the time it takes to complete the algorithm.

When calculating the time-complexity of a certain algorithm or code, you simply look at the number of steps the code would take as the input size grows. For example, the following code segment has an efficiency of O(1). No matter how large the input set is, the algorithm does the same amount of work. Therefore, the runtime is constant.

FIG 6.1: *A program with a time-complexity of O(1)*

```
1    nums = [None] * 1000
2    print(nums[1])
```

The next example has a time-complexity of O(n), which means the runtime will increase proportionally with the input size.

FIG 6.2: *A program with a time-complexity of O(n)*

```
1    nums = [None] * 1000
2    for x in nums:
3        print(x)
```

6.3 LINEAR SEARCH

The simplest way to search a set of elements is using **linear search.** With this process, you compare the **search key**, the value you are looking for, to each value in a set of elements until you find your search key. If we are using the linear search method with an array, we can access each element within an array using its **index**, the position of the element in the array. It is important to keep in mind that the first element of an array starts at index 0, not 1. So, when we use linear search, we begin at index 0 and **traverse** sequentially.

Unlike binary search, which we will discuss later in the chapter, linear search does not require an ordered set of elements. However, linear search often has a greater time-complexity than binary search and requires more memory when the number of elements is large. The time complexity of linear search is O(n) because the amount of work necessary to search the set of elements increases as the number of elements increases.

The following example will demonstrate how we can use linear search to look for a value of 20 in an array. Here is our array:

Index #	0	1	2	3	4	5	6
Value	3	30	5	20	24	12	18

Step 1: The linear search will begin at index 0. Compare the search key, 20, to the value at index 0. Because they are not equal, we move on to the next index.

Index #	0	1	2	3	4	5	6
Value	3	30	5	20	24	12	18

Now, we just repeat the previous step until our search key is found.

Step 2: Compare the key to the value at index 1. They are not equal, so we move on to index 1.

Index #	0	1	2	3	4	5	6
Value	3	30	5	20	24	12	18

Step 3: Compare the key to the value at index 2. They are not equal, so we move on to index 2.

Index #	0	1	2	3	4	5	6
Value	3	30	5	20	24	12	18

Step 4: Compare the key to the value at index 3. They are equal - we have found our key! The value 20 is at index 3.

Index #	0	1	2	3	4	5	6
Value	3	30	5	20	24	12	18

To utilize linear search in Python, our code might look like the following:

FIG 6.3: Implementation of Linear Search

```python
def linear_search(arr, key):
    # checks the value at each index of array to see if it's equal to the key
    for x in arr:
        if x == key:
            return True
    return False


array = [3, 30, 5, 20, 24, 12, 18]
search_key = 20
is_found = linear_search(array, search_key)
print("Searching for", search_key, "...")
if is_found:
    print(search_key, "is found.")
else:
    print(search_key, "is not found.")
```

FIG 6.4: Result of linear search when search key is found

```
Searching for 20 ...
20 is found.
```

Because the search key was found in the set of elements, our program returned "true" and then printed the sentence indicating that the value was found. If the search key was not found, the program would have returned "false" and printed the sentence indicating the value was not found. In the following example, the search key is not in the set of elements, so the program will return "false" and print the sentence indicating it was not found.

FIG 6.5: *Searching for a value that is not present in the array using linear search*

```python
def linear_search(arr, key):
    # checks the value at each index of array to see if it's equal to the key
    for x in arr:
        if x == key:
            return True
    return False


array = [3, 30, 5, 20, 24, 12, 18]
search_key = 50
is_found = linear_search(array, search_key)
print("Searching for", search_key, "...")
if is_found:
    print(search_key, "is found.")
else:
    print(search_key, "is not found.")
```

FIG 6.6: *Result of linear search when search key is not found*

```
Searching for 50 ...
50 is not found.
```

6.4 BINARY SEARCH

While linear search is useful, it is not always the most efficient way to search. In these instances, **binary search** can be used. Binary search is a search method in which you eliminate half of the elements in the search set at a time until you find what you're looking for. The time-complexity of binary search is O(log n) because the time-complexity increases logarithmically as the search set increases in size. Unlike linear search, binary search requires that the set of elements be ordered before you begin your search.

The following example will demonstrate how we can use binary search to find a value in an array. Our search key will be 29, and our set of elements will be ordered from least to greatest. Here is our array:

Index #	0	1	2	3	4	5	6
Value	5	11	12	24	29	36	44

Step 1: To begin a binary search, we start from the middle of the array. In this case, the middle of the array is at index 3.

Index #	0	1	2	3	4	5	6
Value	5	11	12	24	29	36	44

Step 2: This array is sorted so that the values are ordered from least to greatest.So, if the value we are looking for is greater than the value at index 3, it must have an index greater than 3. On the other hand, if the value we are looking for is less than the value at index 3, it must have an index less than 3.

For this example, our search key is 29. The value at index 3 is 24. 29 is greater than 24, we know that the index of our search key must be greater than index 3. Therefore, we can eliminate the values at the indexes less than or equal to index 3. The purged indexes are indicated by the color red.

Index #	0	1	2	3	4	5	6
Value	5	11	12	24	29	36	44

Step 3: Now we have eliminated the bottom half of the array, and we can look at the top half for the value we are searching for. Like we did in the first step, we must identify the middle of the remaining set. This time the middle is at index 5.

Index #	4	5	6
Value	29	36	44

Step 4: The value at index 5 is 36, and we are looking for 29. 36 is greater than 29, so we can eliminate all the values at the indexes greater than or equal to 5.

Index #	4	5	6
Value	29	36	44

We have found our value! 29 is at index 4!

Index #	4
Value	29

It is important to note that the array itself does not change in linear or binary searching. In the above example, for instance, the elements to the left of index 3 are not deleted or removed from the array in any way.

To utilize binary search in Python, our code might look like the following:

FIG 6.7: *Implementation of Binary Search*

```python
def binary_search(arr, key):
    low = 0
    high = len(arr) - 1
    # while loop eliminates half of the searching set at a time until key is found
    while high >= low:
        middle = int((low + high) / 2)
        if arr[middle] == key:
            return True
        if arr[middle] < key:
            low = middle + 1
        if arr[middle] > key:
            high = middle - 1
    return False


array = [5, 11, 12, 24, 29, 36, 44]
search_key = 29
is_found = binary_search(array, search_key)
print("Searching for", search_key, "...")
if is_found:
    print(search_key, "is found.")
else:
    print(search_key, "is not found.")
```

FIG 6.8: *Result of binary search when search key is found*

```
Searching for 29 ...
29 is found.
```

FIG 6.9: *Searching for a value that is not present in the list using binary search*

```python
def binary_search(arr, key):
    low = 0
    high = len(arr) - 1
    # while loop eliminates half of the searching set at a time until key is found
    while high >= low:
        middle = int((low + high) / 2)
        if arr[middle] == key:
            return True
        if arr[middle] < key:
            low = middle + 1
        if arr[middle] > key:
            high = middle - 1
    return False


array = [5, 11, 12, 24, 29, 36, 44]
search_key = 30
is_found = binary_search(array, search_key)
print("Searching for", search_key, "...")
if is_found:
    print(search_key, "is found.")
else:
    print(search_key, "is not found.")
```

FIG 6.10: *Result of binary search when search key is not found*

```
Searching for 30 ...
30 is not found.
```

6.5 DEPTH FIRST SEARCH

Depth first search (DFS) is a traversal and/or searching algorithm used for data structures like trees and graphs. It begins at the root of the graph and traverses deeper into the graph until it must backtrack. It does this for every possible path until every node has been visited, or the search key has been found. The following image is a depiction of the sequence of nodes that would be visited in a tree structure during DFS. A tree only allows us to visit each node once, so the correct term for this diagram would be a graph which would allow cycles.

FIG 6.11: Depth First Search Algorithm on a graph

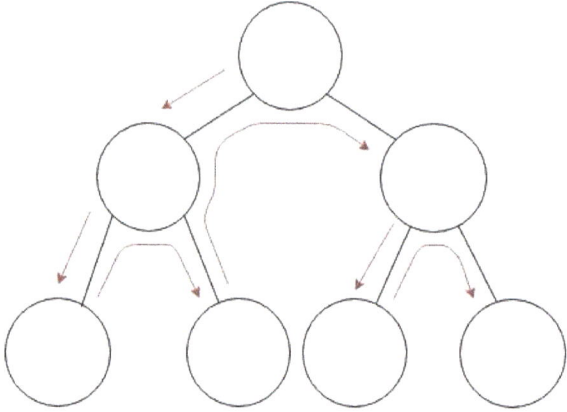

It can be applied to many situations, a notable situation being solving a maze.

In DFS, we search by depth. That is, we traverse the graph to the lowest depth. Our implementation is more of a way to traverse a graph in order to search. However, it can quickly be converted into a search algorithm by adding a comparison. If we were searching with our DFS method, we would check every node to see if it was equal to our search key. We would stop when the key had been found or when every node had been visited. Thus, we will keep track of which edges we have already visited to know where we need to go. Lets create a graph and have the search key be set to 9.

FIG 6.12: Example graph for depth first search

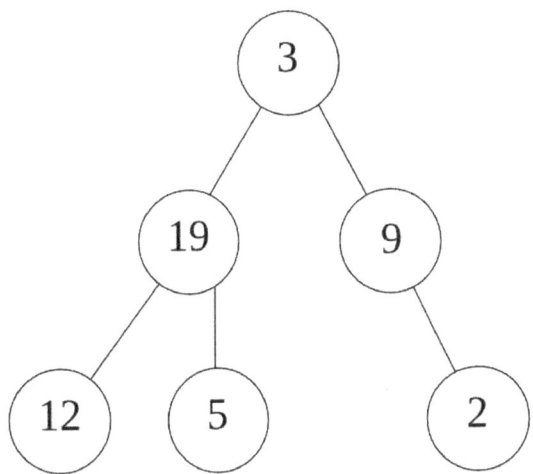

We will indicate the direction of our search with dotted arrows and color the nodes we have already visited as blue and the node we are currently at as grey. First, we begin at the root node whose value is 3.

FIG 6.13: Beginning at root of the graph

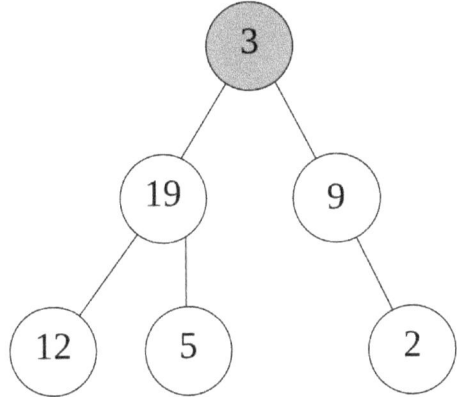

3 is not equal to the key, 9. We check nodes that are connected to the root and find two children nodes. The edges of the two children are pushed into the stack. Since we want to travel to a node, we pop the stack and the first edge that exists is the leftmost child.

FIG 6.14: Traveling along the edge from the root to the left child

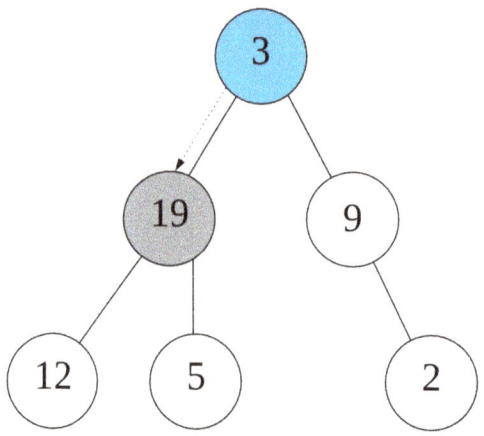

This node contains element 19 and is not equal to the key. While this node is marked as having been visited, the connected edges are pushed into the stack. The two children nodes in level 2 are connected and have not been visited. So we pop the stack and first travel down to the leftmost node in level 2. We must travel down a level to level 2 and we arrive at the left most node.

FIG 6.15: Marking the node 19 as visited and traveling down a connected edge to node 12

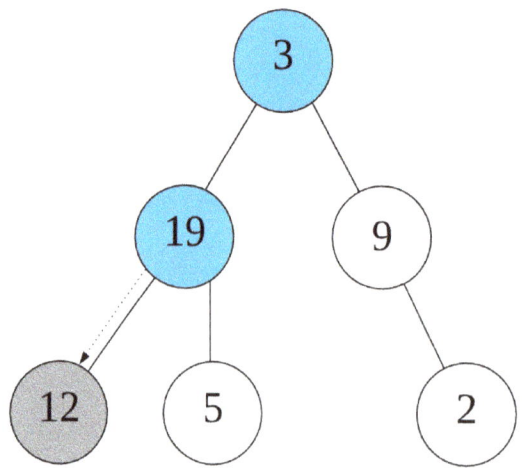

This node contains the element 12, which is not equal to the key. We mark this node as having been visited. Since this node is not connected to any unvisited nodes, we pop the stack. The last thing in our stack is the edge from node, 19, to node 5. The right child node has not been visited so we travel from node 12, up to node 19, down to the node containing element 5.

FIG 6.16: *Marking node 12 as visited and traveling up to the parent before reach the right child node*

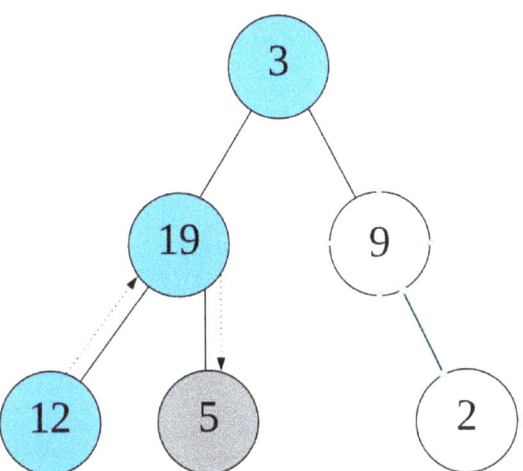

The element 5 is not equal to the key so we mark this node as being visited. There are no connecting edges that have been unvisited, so we pop the stack once again. The remaining edge connects the root to the right child node.

FIG 6.17: *Marking node 5 is visited and traveling up to the root and down to the right child of the root*

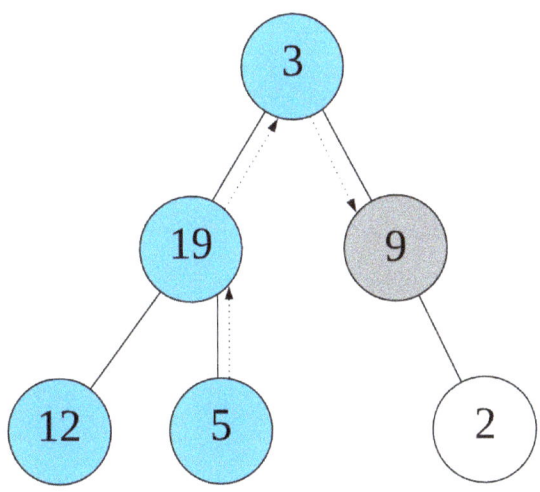

We check if the node, 9, to the key, we have found it! We have found the key within the graph. As you can see with our example, we check the depth of the graph first before every node. Implementing this method would look as follows.

FIG 6.18: *Driver for Depth First Search*

```
42      root_vertex = build_graph()
43      print("Traverse Graph")
44      traverse(root_vertex)
45      print()
46      print("Searching for 9...")
47      vertex_1 = dfs(root_vertex, 9)
48      if vertex_1 is not None:
49          print(vertex_1.data, "is found.")
50      else:
51          print(9, "is not found.")
```

FIG 6.19: *Vertex class*

```
1       class Vertex:
2           def __init__(self, data):
3               self.data = data
4               self.vertex_list = []
5
6           def is_vertex_of(self, vertex):
7               self.vertex_list.append(vertex)
```

FIG 6.20: *Implementing Depth First Search*

```python
    def build_graph():
        vertex1 = Vertex(3)
        vertex2 = Vertex(19)
        vertex3 = Vertex(12)
        vertex4 = Vertex(5)
        vertex5 = Vertex(9)
        vertex6 = Vertex(2)
        vertex1.is_vertex_of(vertex2)
        vertex1.is_vertex_of(vertex5)
        vertex1.is_vertex_of(vertex3)
        vertex2.is_vertex_of(vertex4)
        vertex5.is_vertex_of(vertex6)
        return vertex1


    def dfs(root, search):
        if root.data == search:
            return root
        vertex = None
        for x in root.vertex_list:
            vertex = dfs(x, search)
            if vertex is not None:
                break
        return vertex


    def traverse(root):
        print(root.data, end=" ")
        for x in root.vertex_list:
            traverse(x)
```

FIG 6.21: *Searching for 9 output*

```
Traverse Graph
3 19 5 9 2 12
Searching for 9...
9 is found.
```

Now we will see the results of when the key is not in the tree.

FIG 6.22: *Searching for a value not present in the tree using Depth First Search*

```
42    root_vertex = build_graph()
43    print("Traverse Graph")
44    traverse(root_vertex)
45    print()
46    print("Searching for 1...")
47    vertex_1 = dfs(root_vertex, 1)
48    if vertex_1 is not None:
49        print(vertex_1.data, "is found.")
50    else:
51        print(1, "is not found.")
```

FIG 6.23: *Output for searching for 1*

```
Traverse Graph
3 19 5 9 2 12
Searching for 1...
1 is not found.
```

6.6 BREADTH FIRST SEARCH

Breadth first search (BFS) is a traversal and/or searching algorithm used for data structures like trees and graphs. It begins at the root of the graph and traverses across the breadth of the graph until it reaches the bottom level. It does this for every possible path until every node has been visited, or the search key has been found. The following image is a depiction of the sequence of nodes that would be visited in a tree structure during BFS.

FIG 6.24: Overview of Breadth First Search

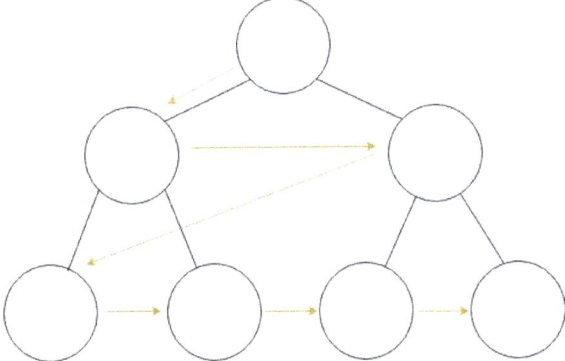

In BFS, we search by breadth. That is, we traverse the graph to the farthest breadth. Our implementation is more of a way to traverse a graph in order to search. However, it can quickly be converted into a search algorithm by adding a comparison. If we were searching with our BFS method, we would check every node to see if it was equal to our search key. We would stop when the key had been found or when every node had been visited. Let's take the same graph from the Depth First Search example and see how differently breadth first search would go about looking for the key 9.

FIG 6.25: *Example tree*

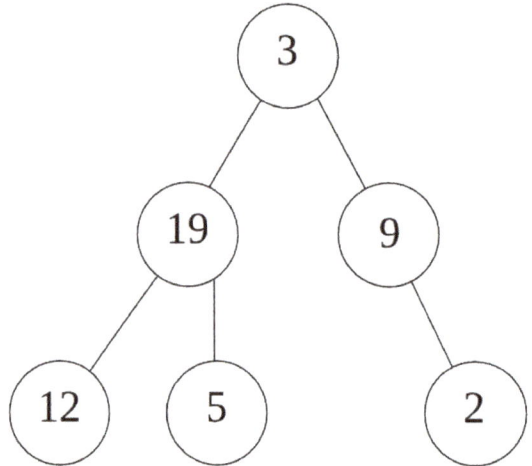

Just like Depth First Search, we begin at the root. We see that the node contains element 3, which is not equal to 9. We mark it as a visited node. There are no neighboring nodes in this level, so we travel down a level and place all the nodes as vertices in level 1 in a queue. The order of nodes entering the queue right now is 19, 9. Since queues follow the rule "first in first out", we visit the node containing 19.

FIG 6.26: *Traveling down the tree to the first node of level 1*

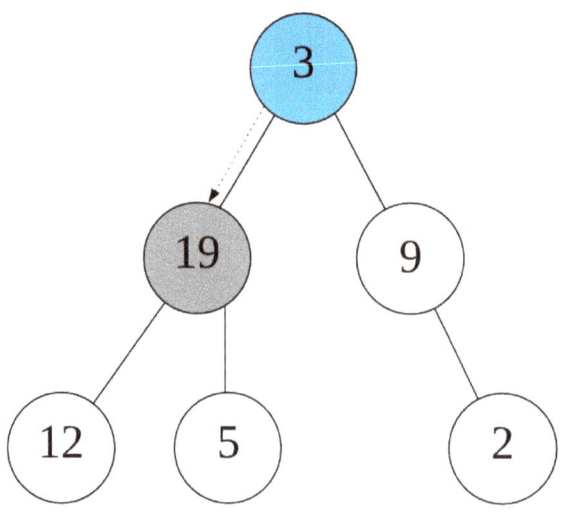

At the node 19 we compare it to the key and dequeue the next node that we will visit. In this case, it is the node containing 9.

FIG 6.27: *Visiting the neighbor node after not finding the key*

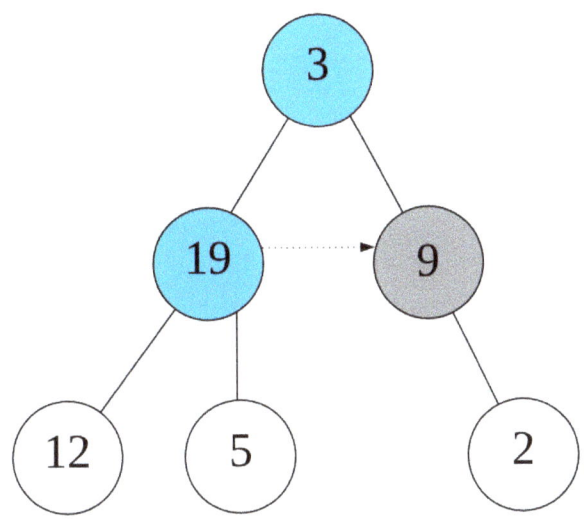

We reach the node containing 9 and compare it to our key. It is equal and we have found it!

FIG 6.28: *Driver for the Breadth First Search*

```
49    root_vertex = build_graph()
50    print("Traverse Graph")
51    traverse(root_vertex)
52    print()
53    print("Searching for 9...")
54    vertex_1 = bfs(root_vertex, 9)
55    if vertex_1 is not None:
56        print(vertex_1.data, "is found.")
57    else:
58        print(9, "is not found.")
```

FIG 6.29: *Vertex class*

```python
class Vertex:
    def __init__(self, data):
        self.data = data
        self.vertex_list = []

    def is_vertex_of(self, vertex):
        self.vertex_list.append(vertex)
```

FIG 6.30: *Implementation of Breadth First Search*

```python
def build_graph():
    vertex1 = Vertex(3)
    vertex2 = Vertex(19)
    vertex3 = Vertex(12)
    vertex4 = Vertex(5)
    vertex5 = Vertex(9)
    vertex6 = Vertex(2)
    vertex1.is_vertex_of(vertex2)
    vertex1.is_vertex_of(vertex5)
    vertex1.is_vertex_of(vertex3)
    vertex2.is_vertex_of(vertex4)
    vertex5.is_vertex_of(vertex6)
    return vertex1


def bfs(root, search):
    queue = [root]
    while not queue:
        vertex = queue.pop(0)
        if vertex.data == search:
            return vertex
        for x in vertex.vertex_list:
            queue.append(x)
    return None
```

```python
    def traverse(root):
        traverse_order = []
        queue = [root]
        while len(queue) > 0:
            vertex = queue.pop(0)
            traverse_order.append(vertex)
            for x in vertex.vertex_list:
                queue.append(x)
        while len(traverse_order) > 0:
            vertex = traverse_order.pop(0)
            print(vertex.data, end=" ")
```

FIG 6.31 *Results of Breadth First Search looking for key 9*

```
Traverse Graph
3 19 9 12 5 2
Searching for 9...
9 is found.
```

Now we will see what happens we use breadth first search for a key that does not exist in the tree

FIG 6.32: *Driver class for an example in which the key does not exist in the graph*

```
49      root_vertex = build_graph()
50      print("Traverse Graph")
51      traverse(root_vertex)
52      print()
53      print("Searching for 1...")
54      vertex_1 = bfs(root_vertex, 1)
55      if vertex_1 is not None:
56          print(vertex_1.data, "is found.")
57      else:
58          print(1, "is not found.")
```

FIG 6.33: *Results when key is not in the graph*

```
Traverse Graph
3 19 9 12 5 2
Searching for 1...
1 is not found.
```

Now if you have noticed with this particular graph and key, it did not require us to travel to as many nodes as it did with the depth first search. However, we can show how it is dependent on the graph and key by showing how the two methods would look for the key 12 in the graph.

FIG 6.34: *Comparing breadth first search and depth first search*

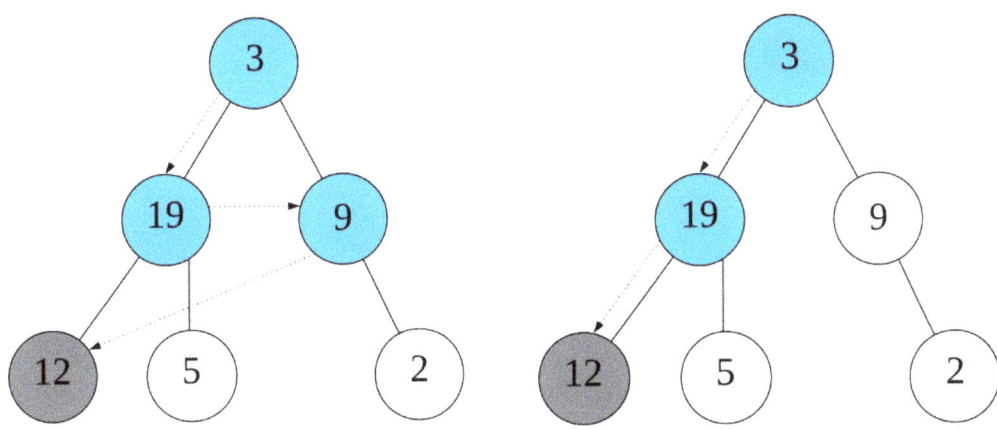

In this instance depth first search, shown on the right, did not require traveling to as many nodes to find the key. Since breadth first search uses a queue data structure, it is slower in that aspect.

Chapter 7 Additional Topics

CHAPTER CONTENTS

7.1 Max and Min Heap
7.2 Dijkstra's Shortest Path Algorithm
7.3 Minimax Algorithm
7.4 Alpha Beta Pruning

7.1 MAX AND MIN HEAP

Before we jump into a new data structure, let's define some terms. Diagrams of trees have already been shown to describe the processes of other algorithms. While in trees, each node could have as many child nodes as desired, in a **binary tree** each node can have at most two children nodes. Thus, each node can either have 0, 1, or 2 children. However, if a tree were to be created in which every node has 2 children nodes except the terminal nodes and each level had 2^l number of nodes where l is the level number except for the final level, it would be called a **complete binary tree.** For instance, level 1 of a 3 level complete binary tree should have 2 nodes.

Thus, a **heap** is a data structure in which the data structure is a complete binary tree. It is often referred to as a nearly complete binary tree as the final level of the tree does not have the maximum number of nodes possible. Simple. A max heap will have the root of the tree contain the highest value compared to its children. A min heap will have the root of the tree contain the smallest value compared to its children. Below are two examples of a simple max heap and min heap that shows how the values are arranged.

FIG 7.1: Complete Binary Trees of Min Heap and Max Heap

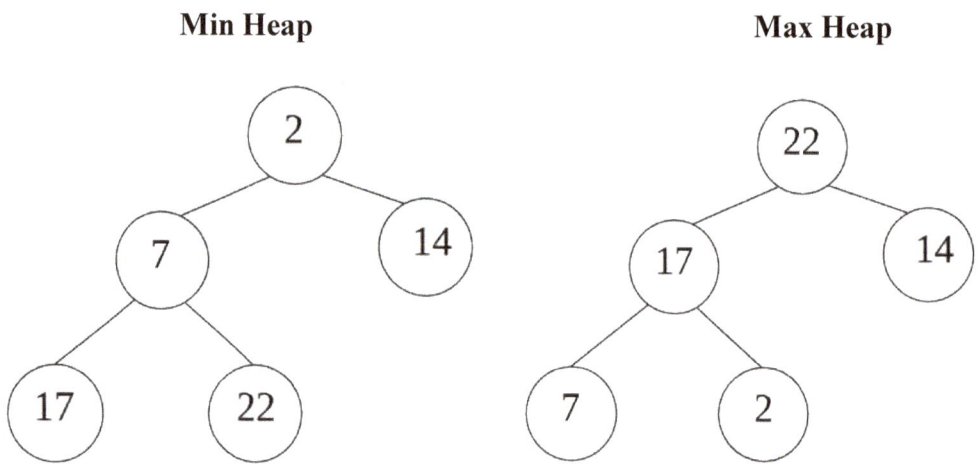

In the min heap, the parent node is always smaller than the children nodes. In the max heap, the parent node is always larger than the children nodes. As well, with this example you can see how each node either has 2 children nodes or no children nodes.

INSERTING INTO A HEAP

Creating a heap, it is best to see it as an array that can be shown as a complete binary tree. Let's just focus on creating a max heap. The method will be called

Insert in which we will add data to the end of an array. Lets begin Just making the max heap object. We will show this as an array and complete binary tree. Right now, there is nothing in the array and nothing in the complete binary tree.

Index #
Value

○

Now we will call the Insert method and place 5 into the end of the array.

Index #	0
Value	5

(5)

Now, let's just build up the tree by repeating the same process. Let's insert the data 3 into the back of the array and as a child of the root.

After each insertion we will compare the current newly inserted node with the parent node until we reach the root to see if we need to swap any of the elements. As this is a max heap, we want the parent node to always be larger than the child. In this case, we only need to compare the newly inserted child with the root. We see that the new child is smaller than the parent and does not need to switch.

To see the process in effect, let's call the method Insert and insert the data 17 to the end of the array. Now the array is able to be translated into the tree by reading it through levels. Because of the formula 2^l, we know how many nodes are in each level. The first element in the array will be the root of level 0. The element of index 1 of the array will become the left child in level 1 and element of index 2 will become the right child of level 1. So on and so forth. Thus, this is what will happen after we insert 17.

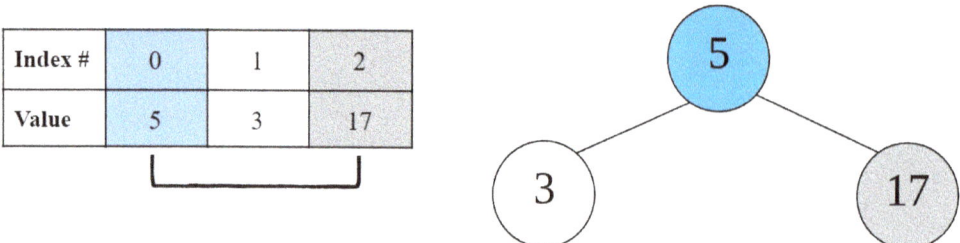

Now we compare the newly inserted node colored grey with the parent node colored blue. In this instance, the child node is larger and thus needs to be switched. Index 0 and index 2 of the array will be switched while the parent node will be switched with the right child in the tree.

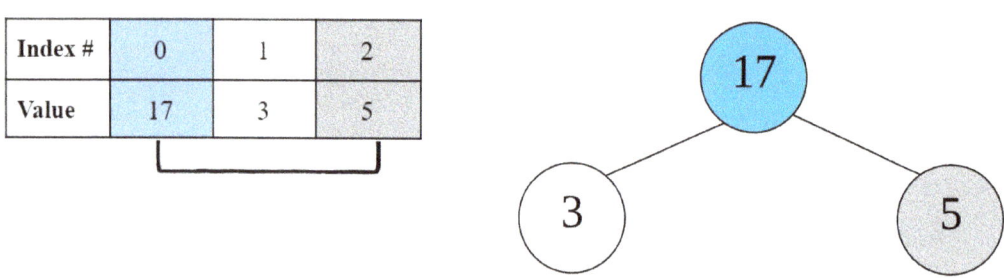

Let's use the Insert method once again and add the number 10 into the array.

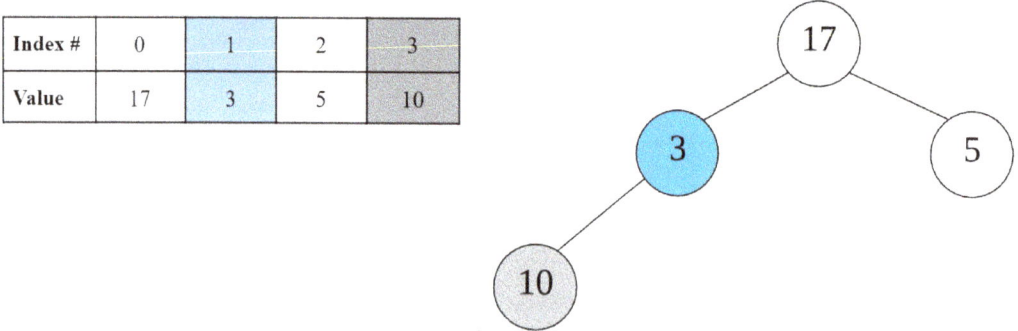

The newly inserted node is the left child to the node that contains the integer 3. Now that it has been added, we start comparing the child node to the parent. Since the child is larger than the parent, we swap.

Index #	0	1	2	3
Value	17	10	5	3

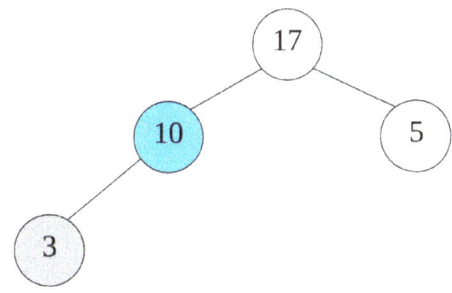

ust to check, we compare the node 10 with the parent node 17. As it is smaller than the parent node, we do not need to swap and this location is kept. As well the child node is smaller so the location is good. For this example, we will Insert one more integer: 84.

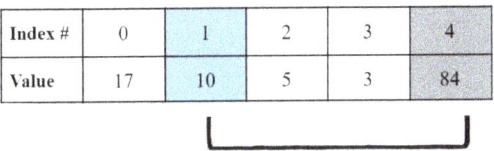

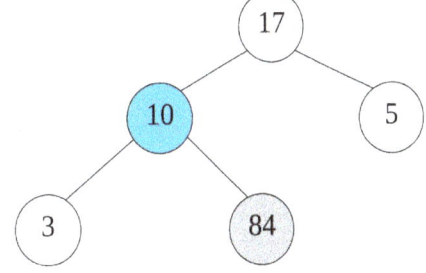

Comparing the inserted element 84 to the parent node, we see that we need to switch them. So 84 becomes the parent node while 10 becomes the right child.

Index #	0	1	2	3	4
Value	17	84	5	3	10

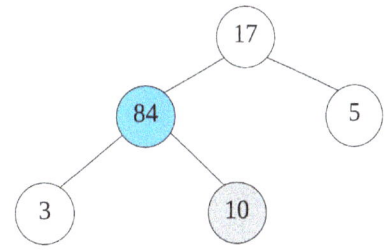

Having swapped them, we must check again if the parent node of 84 is larger. Comparing 84 and 17, we see that we must swap the node again and 84 becomes the root.

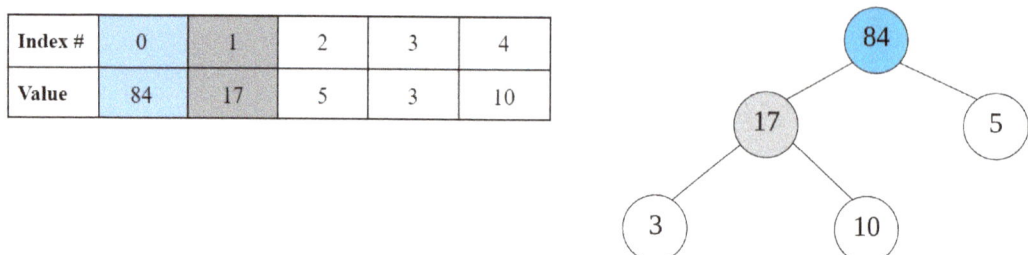

Now we have to check that the children node of the swapped node is smaller and they are. At this instance all parent nodes are larger than children nodes.

Now that you understand how the heap is formed as new elements are added using the Insert D method, we will express what the final max tree would look like if these integers were added: 5, 3, 17, 10, 84, 19, 6, 22, 9.

FIG 7.2: *Completed Binary Tree and Array representation of a Max Heap*

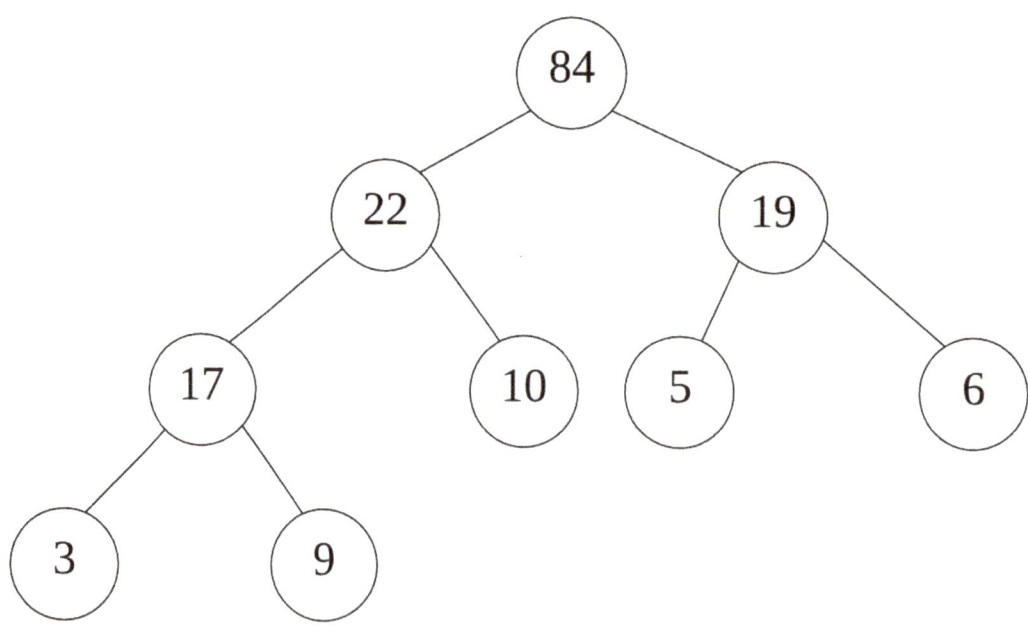

Index	0	1	2	3	4	5	6	7	8
Value	84	22	19	17	10	5	6	3	9

REMOVING MAX FROM A MAX HEAP

We are able to remove the max element from the heap as we know that the max element is the root. Taking the heap we have just created, we swap the root with the last element of the heap. In the array we are switching the lowest index element with the highest index element. It is easiest to remove the last element of the array as it would not disrupt the other indexes and elements. So 84 is moved from index 0 to index 8 and removed.

Index	0	1	2	3	4	5	6	7	8
Value	9	22	19	17	10	5	6	3	84

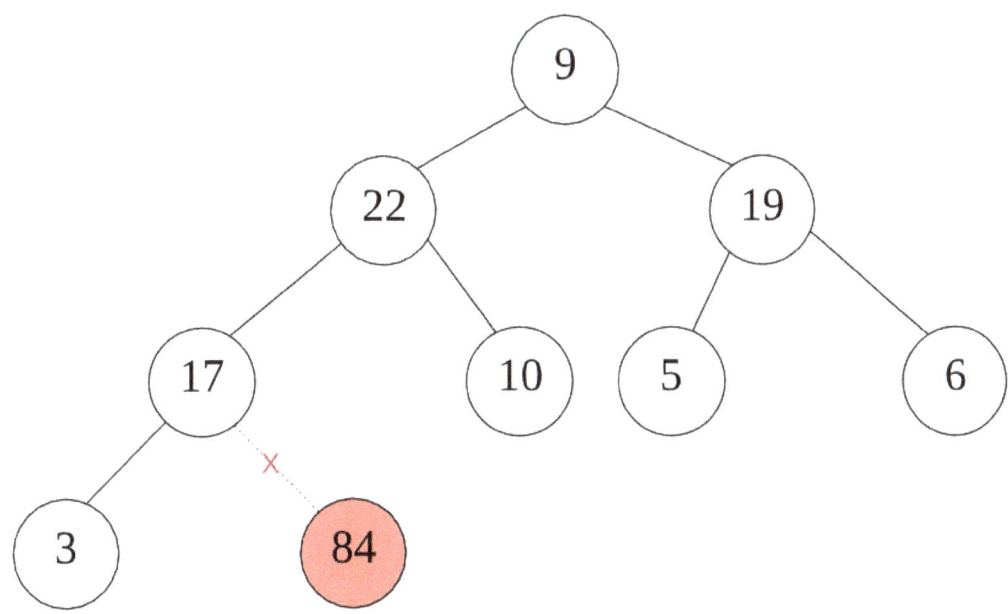

The only issue now is that the entire heap is unsorted. There we are going to use a method called MaxHeapify to compare the parent and child nodes similar to what we did with the Insert method to see if we need to switch. We will compare the root, 9, with the left child node, 22.

Index	0	1	2	3	4	5	6	7
Value	9	22	19	17	10	5	6	3

As the child node is larger, we will switch the child and the parent. The following tree shows the results.

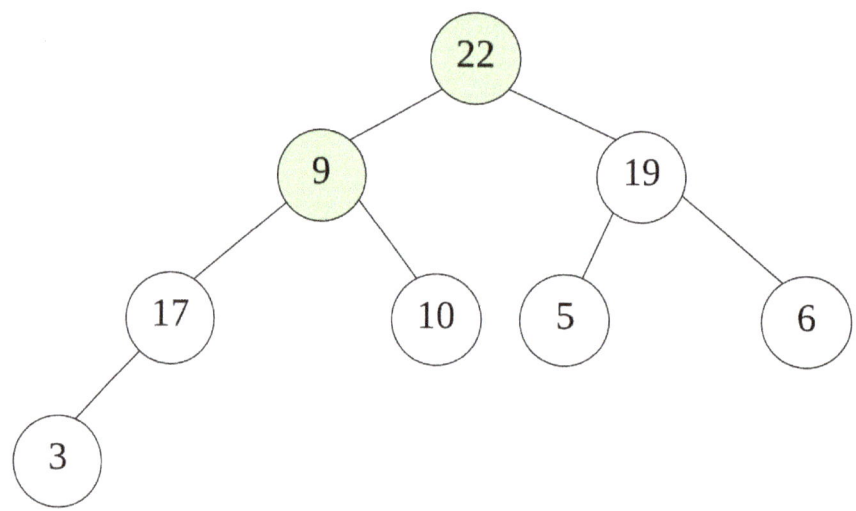

As shown with the array below, the next step will be comparing the newly moved node 9 with its left child which has the element 17.

Index	0	1	2	3	4	5	6	7
Value	22	9	19	17	10	5	6	3

The child node, 17, is larger than the parent node, 9. Thus we must switch the nodes. The following tree shows the results of the switch.

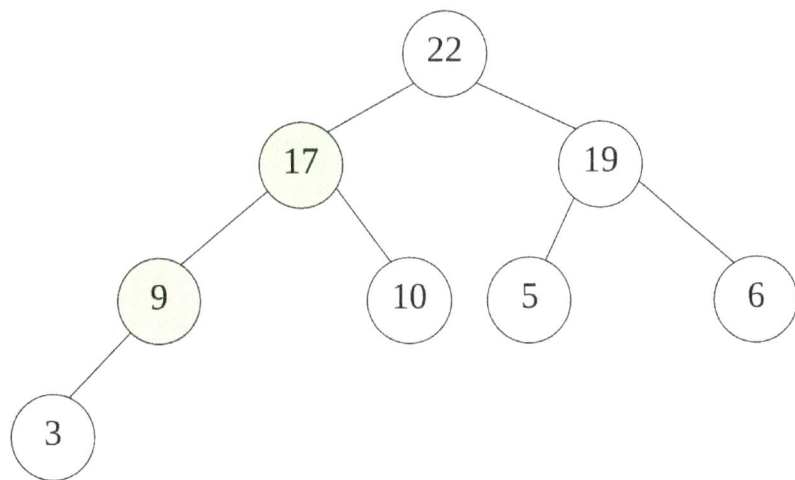

We compare the newly moved node, 9, with its child node. In this case the child node contains the element 3 as shown by the array below.

Index	0	1	2	3	4	5	6	7
Value	22	17	19	9	10	5	6	3

Now if we were to compare every single parent node with the child node, we see that the heap has been reorganized. While not shown, each parent node will be compared to their child nodes. However, we can see that it is completed now.

FIG 7.3: Completed Binary Tree and Array representation after removing max element

Index	0	1	2	3	4	5	6	7
Value	22	17	19	9	10	5	6	3

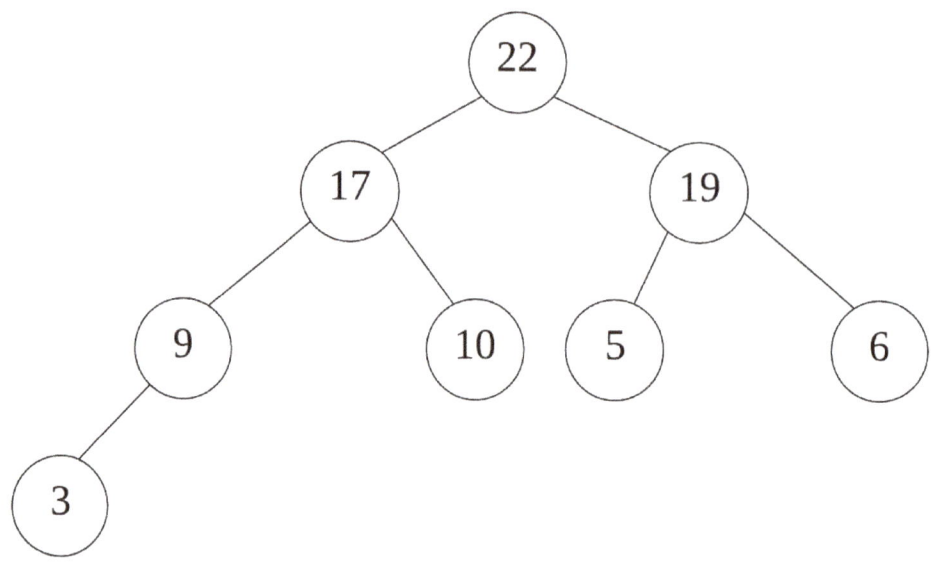

REMOVE ELEMENT FROM A MAX HEAP

Once you understand how to remove the maximum value of the heap, it is very easy to remove any element from the heap. Continuing with the same heap, let's say we want to remove the element 17. As you are most likely familiar with from other searching methods, we are going to traverse the array and find the index of the element. Here it is just like the previous method, we will switch it with the final element, remove the final index, and reorganize the array once again. Here we find the element 17 is at index 1. We will switch index 1 with index 7.

Index	0	1	2	3	4	5	6	7
Value	22	3	19	9	10	5	6	17

The index 7 is removed from the array. Now is the same MaxHeafy method of reorganizing the array by checking the parent nodes against the children nodes. As you are most likely an expert of this method by now, let's jump to the end result. This will be the final array.

Index	0	1	2	3	4	5	6
Value	22	10	19	9	3	5	6

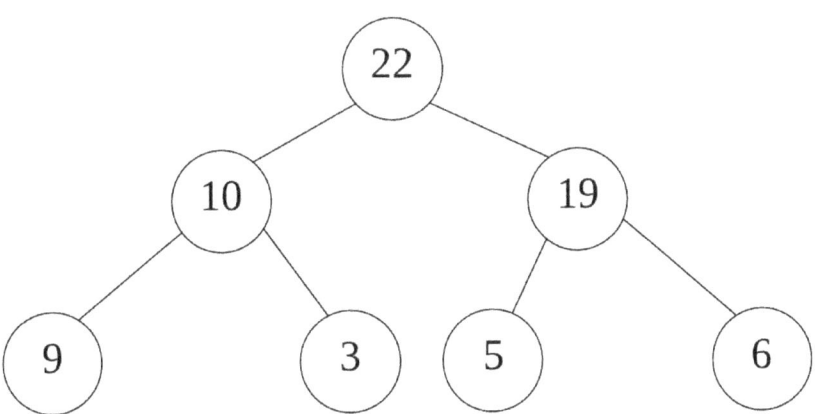

The implementation of all three of these methods will look like the following. Below, the index starts at 1 rather than 0 to simplify the implementation.

FIG 7.4: *Inserting elements into Max Heap*

```python
91      if __name__ == "__main__":
92          print("The Max Heap is ")
93          max_heap = MaxHeap(15)
94          max_heap.insert(5)
95          max_heap.insert(3)
96          max_heap.insert(17)
97          max_heap.insert(10)
98          max_heap.insert(84)
99          max_heap.insert(19)
100         max_heap.insert(6)
101         max_heap.insert(22)
102         max_heap.insert(9)
103
104         max_heap.display_heap()
105         print("The max val is", max_heap.extract_max())
106         max_heap.display_heap()
107         print("Removing 17 from heap...")
108         max_heap.remove(17)
109         max_heap.display_heap()
```

FIG 7.5: *Implementation of MaxHeap Class*

```python
1    import sys
2
3
4    class MaxHeap:
5        def __init__(self, max_size):
6            self.max_size = max_size
7            self.current_size = 0
8            self.max_heap_tree = [0] * (max_size + 1)
9            self.max_heap_tree[0] = sys.maxsize
10           self.ROOT = 1
11
12       # returns the position of the parent
13       def parent(self, position):
14           return position // 2
```

```python
    # returns the position of the left child
    def left_child(self, position):
        return 2 * position

    # returns the position of the right child
    def right_child(self, position):
        return (2 * position) + 1

    # determines whether the node is a leaf
    def is_leaf(self, position):
        if (self.current_size // 2) <= position <= self.current_size:
            return True
        return False

    # element from the heap
    def extract_max(self):
        popped = self.max_heap_tree[self.ROOT]
        self.max_heap_tree[self.ROOT] = self.max_heap_tree[self.current_size]
        self.current_size -= 1
        self.max_heapify(self.ROOT)
        return popped
```

```python
# removes a specific node from the heap
def remove(self, element):
    index = 0
    for x in range(1, self.current_size + 1):
        if self.max_heap_tree[x] == element:
            index = x
    if index != 0:
        popped = self.max_heap_tree[index]
        self.swap(self.current_size, index)
        self.current_size -= 1
        self.max_heapify(index)
        return popped
    return 0

# swap two nodes
def swap(self, fposition, sposition):
    temp = self.max_heap_tree[fposition]
    self.max_heap_tree[fposition] = self.max_heap_tree[sposition]
    self.max_heap_tree[sposition] = temp
```

```python
    # inserts a node in the heap
    def insert(self, element):
        if self.current_size < self.max_size:
            self.current_size += 1
            self.max_heap_tree[self.current_size] = element
            element_index = self.current_size
            while self.max_heap_tree[element_index] > self.max_heap_tree[self.parent(element_index)]:
                self.swap(element_index, self.parent(element_index))
                element_index = self.parent(element_index)

    # rearrange the heap
    def max_heapify(self, position):
        if self.is_leaf(position):
            return
        if self.max_heap_tree[position] < self.max_heap_tree[self.left_child(position)] or self.max_heap_tree[position] < self.max_heap_tree[self.right_child(position)]:
            if self.max_heap_tree[self.left_child(position)] > self.max_heap_tree[self.right_child(position)]:

                self.swap(position, self.left_child(position))
                self.max_heapify(self.left_child(position))
            else:
                self.swap(position, self.right_child(position))
                self.max_heapify(self.right_child(position))

```

```
80          # display the heap
81          def display_heap(self):
82              for i in range(1, (self.current_size // 2) + 1):
83                  print(" Parent:", self.max_heap_tree[i],
       end=" ")
84                  if (2 * i) <= self.current_size:
85                      print(" Left Child:",
       self.max_heap_tree[2 * i], end=" ")
86                  if (2 * i + 1) <= self.current_size:
87                      print(" Right Child:",
       self.max_heap_tree[2 * i + 1], end=" ")
88                  print()
```

FIG 7.6: *Output of methods for Heap*

```
The Max Heap is
 Parent: 84  Left Child: 22  Right Child: 19
 Parent: 22  Left Child: 17  Right Child: 10
 Parent: 19  Left Child: 5  Right Child: 6
 Parent: 17  Left Child: 3  Right Child: 9
The max val is 84
 Parent: 22  Left Child: 17  Right Child: 19
 Parent: 17  Left Child: 9  Right Child: 10
 Parent: 19  Left Child: 5  Right Child: 6
 Parent: 9  Left Child: 3
Removing 17 from heap...
 Parent: 22  Left Child: 10  Right Child: 19
 Parent: 10  Left Child: 9  Right Child: 3
 Parent: 19  Left Child: 5  Right Child: 6
```

We showed the implementation of inserting an element, removing the max element, and removing a given element from a max heap. To implement these processes in min heap, it would be almost identical except we will check that the parent node must be smaller than its connecting children nodes. As well, it would attempt to remove the min element except the max element.

7.2 DIJKSTRA'S SHORTEST PATH ALGORITHM

The shortest path algorithms are implemented to perform a wide variety of tasks including finding the shortest navigation route, shipping route, or even IP route. Shortest path algorithms are essential algorithms applied to real situations that find the shortest path between a **root vertex** and a **destination vertex** on a graph. The algorithms accomplish this by comparing all of the different paths from the root to the destination and choosing the minimum. On a graph, **vertices** are connected by **edges**, or paths. The goal of the algorithm is to find the shortest path between the root and the destination, so the sum of the **weights** of the edges between visited vertices must be at a minimum. The weight of an edge represents the cost of traveling on that path. You can think of cost as in the time it takes to drive from point A to B or how much money it takes to use the toll road.

FIG 7.7: Graph example of Shortest Path Algorithm

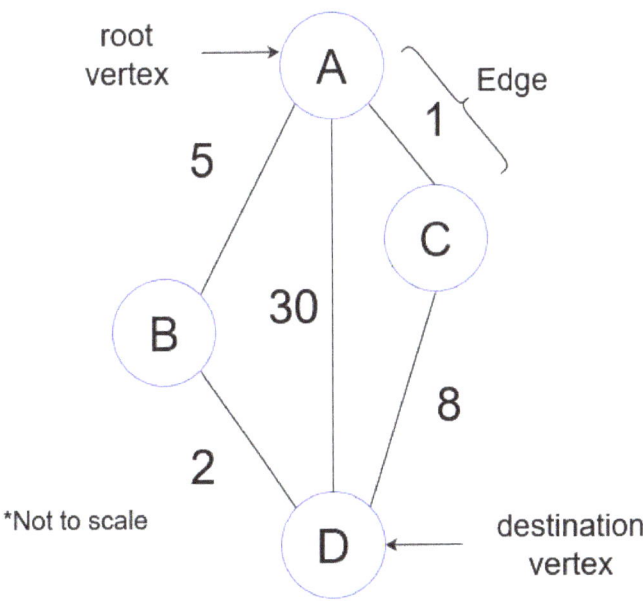

In the above example, vertex A is the root vertex, and vertex D is the destination vertex. Therefore, we are trying to find the shortest path from vertex A to vertex D. In this case, we will define shortest by the smallest total weight value. The vertices on the graph are connected by edges. The shortest path from vertex A to vertex D is from A→ B → D. In that case, the sum of the weights of the edges between visited vertices is 7.

There are several methods we can use to find the shortest path, but in this chapter, we will use a slightly modified version of **Dijkstra's algorithm.** Rather than using multiple arrays to keep track of visited and unvisited vertices as the traditional Dijkstra's algorithm does, we will use a priority queue to eliminate the need for extra data structures and increase the speed of the algorithm.

Dijkstra's algorithm models points on a graph using the Vertex and Edge classes. The vertices on the graph are objects of the class Vertex, and the edges are objects of the class Edge.

First, let's take a closer look at the Vertex class. Each Vertex object has an array of adjacent edges, a name, a parent, and a variable to store the current shortest path.

FIG 7.8: Vertex class

```python
import sys


class Vertex:
    def __init__(self, name):
        self.name = name
        self.parent = None
        self.shortest_path = sys.maxsize
        self.adjacencies = []
```

The array named adjacencies stores every edge adjacent to the Vertex object. The String vertexName holds the name of the Vertex object, and the Vertex parent is a reference to the Vertex object's "parent," or the Vertex object that came before in the path sequence. If the Vertex object is the root vertex, its parent is null.

To recover the sequence of vertices that make up the shortest path, we use the variable shortestPath to store the sum of the weights of the edges that lead to the current shortest path. This variable is initially set to infinity because the algorithm continuously recalculates the distance from the root to each vertex in the graph until the shortest distance from the root to each vertex is found.

Now, let's take a look at the Edge class.

FIG 7.9: *Edge class*

```
12      class Edge:
13          def __init__(self, target, weight):
14              self.target = target
15              self.weight = weight
```

The Vertex target represents the vertex the Edge object leads to. The integer weight stores the cost it takes to travel that edge.

With some background on the Vertex and Edge classes, we can now construct Vertex and Edge objects in the driver.

FIG 7.10: *Driver class creating 6 vertices*

```python
        if __name__ == "__main__":
            # construct vertices
            n1 = Vertex("A")
            n2 = Vertex("B")
            n3 = Vertex("C")
            n4 = Vertex("D")
            n5 = Vertex("E")
            n6 = Vertex("F")

            # initialize their edges
            n1.adjacencies.append(Edge(n2, 15))
            n1.adjacencies.append(Edge(n3, 2))
            n1.adjacencies.append(Edge(n6, 30))

            n2.adjacencies.append(Edge(n1, 15))
            n2.adjacencies.append(Edge(n4, 1))

            n3.adjacencies.append(Edge(n1, 2))
            n3.adjacencies.append(Edge(n5, 7))

            n4.adjacencies.append(Edge(n2, 1))
            n4.adjacencies.append(Edge(n6, 3))

            n5.adjacencies.append(Edge(n3, 7))
            n5.adjacencies.append(Edge(n6, 8))

            n6.adjacencies.append(Edge(n1, 30))
            n6.adjacencies.append(Edge(n4, 3))
            n6.adjacencies.append(Edge(n5, 8))
```

A visual representation of the objects constructed in the driver above might look like the following:

FIG 7.11: *Visual representation of vertices and edges*

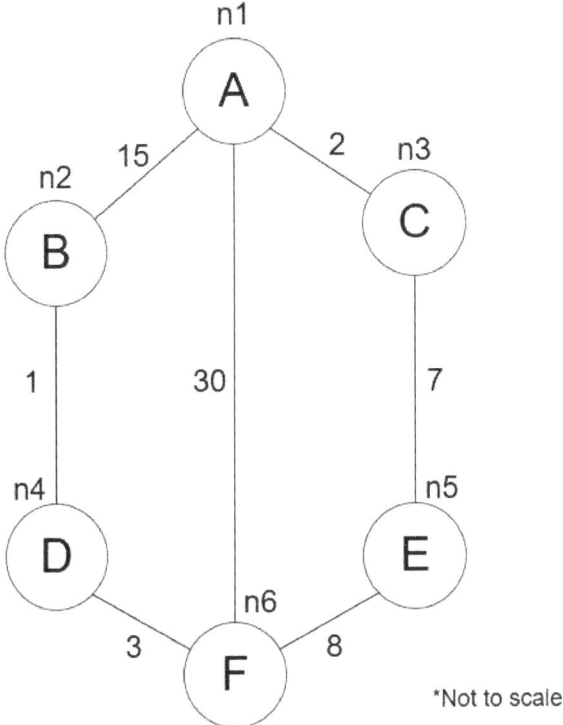

As you can see, each vertex has a name and its own set of edges that lead to adjacent vertices.

Besides the Vertex and Edge classes, we will also use the Stack, PriorityQueue, Node, and LinkedList classes to implement the algorithm. Though the concepts of these data structures remain the same, we have slightly changed their implementations to adapt to the situation at hand. Furthermore, the data structures will not have explicitly defined constructors. With Python, a **default constructor** will be automatically created if a constructor is not explicitly defined in a class. A default constructor is a constructor with no parameters that either calls the default constructor of the superclass or nullifies any unassigned variables in the class if there is no superclass.

Let's look at the Node and LinkedList classes. An object of the LinkedList class will be a linked list of Vertex objects. Unlike the linked lists we explored in Chapter Three, the linked list in this chapter will have a head that points to an empty node. In other words, the node's data variable is null. This is made possible with the additional constructor in our Node class with no parameters that sets data and next to null. Now, upon the construction of a LinkedList object, there is one element in the linked list - the empty node. This version of implementing the LinkedList class with the additional constructor is popular among many professionals and professors, so it is beneficial to know.

FIG 7.12: *Node class*

```
18    class Node:
19        def __init__(self, data):
20            self.data = data
21            self.next = None
```

FIG 7.13: *LinkedList class*

```
24    class LinkedList:
25        def __init__(self):
26            self.head = Node(None)
27
28        def is_empty(self):
29            return self.head.next is None
30
31        def insert_front(self, data):
32            new_node = Node(data)
33            new_node.next = self.head.next
34            self.head.next = new_node
35
36        def insert_end(self, data):
37            new_node = Node(data)
38            temp = self.head
39            while temp.next is not None:
40                temp = temp.next
41            temp.next = new_node
42
43        def remove_front(self):
44            if self.head.next is not None:
45                temp = self.head.next
46                self.head.next = temp.next
47                return temp.data
48            else:
```

```
                print("empty")
                return None

        def remove_end(self):
            prev = None
            temp = self.head
            while temp.next is not None:
                prev = temp
                temp = temp.next
            prev.next = None
            return temp.data

        def print(self, data_structure):
            if self.head.next is None:
                print("The", data_structure, "is empty.")
                return
            temp = self.head
            while temp.next is not None:
                print(temp.next.data.name + "-Distance cost =", temp.next.data.shortest_path)
                temp = temp.next
```

Here's our Stack class. The purpose of the stack is to hold the sequence of the vertices in the shortest path. The destination vertex is at the bottom of the stack, and the root vertex is at the top. When we later pop elements off of the stack, we will have the order of the vertices in the shortest path.

FIG 7.14: Stack class

```
71    class Stack(LinkedList):
72        def __init__(self):
73            super().__init__()
74
75        def push(self, data):
76            self.insert_front(data)
77
78        def pop(self):
79            return self.remove_front
80
81        def display(self):
82            super().print("Stack")
```

Here's our PriorityQueue class. Our PriorityQueue class also extends the LinkedList class and holds vertices organized by their priority. The vertices' priorities are determined by the value of their shortest_path variable. The vertex with the shortest path is sent to the front of the queue and the vertex with the longest path is sent to the back.

FIG 7.15: PriorityQueue class

```python
class PriorityQueue(LinkedList):
    def __init__(self):
        super().__init__()

    def enqueue(self, data):
        new_node = Node(data)
        if self.head.next is None:
            self.head.next = new_node
        else:
            temp = self.head.next
            prev = self.head
            not_found = True
            while not_found and temp is not None:
                if temp.data.shortest_path <= data.shortest_path:
                    prev = temp
                    temp = temp.next
                else:
                    not_found = False
                    prev.next = new_node
                    new_node.next = temp
            if not_found and temp is None:
                prev.next = new_node

    def dequeue(self):
        return super().remove_front()

    def display(self):
        super().print("Priority Queue")
```

FIG 7.16: *Dijkstra Algorithm*

```
115    # accepts the root vertex
116    def calculate_shortest_path(source):
117        queue = PriorityQueue()
118
119        # sets the root's shortest path to 0
120        source.shortest_path = 0
121        queue.enqueue(source)
122
123        while not queue.is_empty():
124            u = queue.dequeue()
125            # executes for every edge adjacent to u
126            for edge in u.adjacencies:
127                v = edge.target
128                # executes if shortest path from u to v is shorter than v's shortest path
129                if (edge.weight + u.shortest_path) < v.shortest_path:
130                    # update shortest path
131                    v.shortest_path = edge.weight + u.shortest_path
132                    # update parent
133                    v.parent = u
134                    # add v to priority queue
135                    queue.enqueue(v)
```

Dijkstra's algorithm finds the shortest path from the root vertex to every other vertex. This is done by comparing each vertex's shortest_path variable. The root starts with a shortest_path of 0, because that is where we start. Every other vertex has a shortest_path of infinity. If a shorter path to a vertex is found, we update the shortest_path variable. We also update the parent variable so we know which vertex we came from. Because we know each vertex's parent, we can reconstruct the sequence of the shortest path to each vertex by traversing through its parents.

The procedure for finding the shortest path is as follows:

1) In the driver, we construct all of our vertices and edges. The shortest_path variable of each vertex is set to infinity
2) We begin at the root vertex and try to reach the destination vertex in the shortest path possible. We call the Dijkstra algorithm and pass the root vertex as an argument. The algorithm will find the shortest path from the root to every vertex in the graph.
3) The algorithm starts with the creation of a priority queue
4) We set the root vertex's shortest_path variable to 0 and add it to our priority queue. We will find the shortest path from the vertex in the graph.
5) While the priority queue isn't empty…
    a) We will dequeue a vertex "u" from the priority queue. This is the vertex with the shortest path
    b) For every edge is u's array of adjacent edges…
        i) The target vertex of each edge will be called "v"
            (1) if there is a shorter path to v through u
                (a) we will update v's shortest_path variable to equal u's shortest_path variable plus the weight of the edge
                (b) we will set v's parent to u. This will allow us to reconstruct the shortest path later, as we now know which vertex we came from to reach v
                (c) lastly, we will add v to the priority queue
            (2) If there is not a shorter path from u to v, we do nothing
6) The loop ends when the priority queue is empty, or when the shortest path from the root to each vertex has been found
7) Now Dijkstra's algorithm has found the shortest path to every vertex in the graph. To know the sequence of the shortest path from our root to a specific destination, we can work backwards
8) To reconstruct the sequence of the vertices from our root to our destination, we start at our destination and create a temporary variable that points to the vertex's parent. We traverse through the path like the way we would traverse a linked list. Because each vertex has a reference to its parent in the same way that a node has a reference to the next node, we can loop through the parents until we reach the root. We visit each parent, add it to the stack, and move the variable's pointer to the temporary variable's parent.
9) We repeat this process until we reach the root vertex, which does not have a parent

10) When all the vertices have been pushed onto the stack with the destination at the bottom and the root at the top, we can pop off the vertices and print the min order to give us our shortest path

Here is our complete driver.

FIG 7.17: *Driver that creates six vertices, assigns them edges, and finds the shortest path from vertex B to vertex F*

```
138    if __name__ == "__main__":
139        # construct vertices
140        n1 = Vertex("A")
141        n2 = Vertex("B")
142        n3 = Vertex("C")
143        n4 = Vertex("D")
144        n5 = Vertex("E")
145        n6 = Vertex("F")
146
147        # initialize their edges
148        n1.adjacencies.append(Edge(n2, 15))
149        n1.adjacencies.append(Edge(n3, 2))
150        n1.adjacencies.append(Edge(n6, 30))
151
152        n2.adjacencies.append(Edge(n1, 15))
153        n2.adjacencies.append(Edge(n4, 1))
154
155        n3.adjacencies.append(Edge(n1, 2))
156        n3.adjacencies.append(Edge(n5, 7))
157
158        n4.adjacencies.append(Edge(n2, 1))
159        n4.adjacencies.append(Edge(n6, 3))
160
161        n5.adjacencies.append(Edge(n3, 7))
162        n5.adjacencies.append(Edge(n6, 8))
```

```
            n6.adjacencies.append(Edge(n1, 30))
            n6.adjacencies.append(Edge(n4, 3))
            n6.adjacencies.append(Edge(n5, 8))

            vertex_source = n2
            destination = n6

            calculate_shortest_path(vertex_source)

            node_stack = Stack()
            node_stack.push(destination)
            parent_node = destination.parent

            while parent_node is not None:
                node_stack.push(parent_node)
                parent_node = parent_node.parent

            node_stack.display()
```

FIG 7.18: Result of creating six vertices, assigning them edges, and finding the shortest path from vertex B to vertex F

```
B-Distance cost = 0
D-Distance cost = 1
F-Distance cost = 4
```

As you can see, the shortest path from vertex B to vertex F is from B to D and then F. Note that the sum of the weights of the edges between visited vertices was 4. Therefore, the shortest path cost 4 units.

7.3 MINIMAX ALGORITHM

The **Minimax Algorithm** determines the best appropriate action for a player to choose given the opponent plays optimally. Often used in gaming situations involving two players, this algorithm accomplishes the task by mapping all possible player outcomes and assigning each position a value corresponding to the desirability for the player. The value is determined by the programmer in which high values indicate an advantage for the player and lower values indicate an advantage for the opponent. It is assumed the opponent will always choose the move/position that has a lower value which benefits the opponent.

A directed graph is used to express the connections between the possible moves. The possible positions are designated by nodes while the arrows represent the moves of the player and the opponent. This particular type of directed graph is known specifically as a game tree.

FIG 7.19: A game tree expressing the Minimax Algorithm for a game with two moves after each position

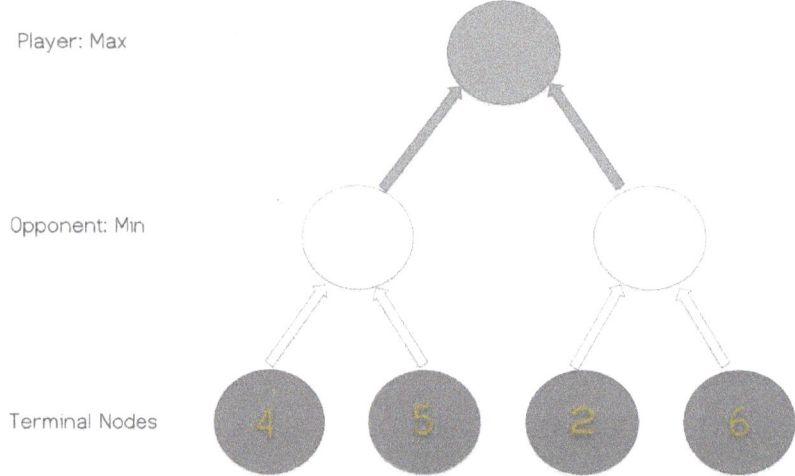

This game tree expresses a game in which there exists only two possible moves after each position. The root of the tree represents the player striving for the maximum value's first move. The first level of the tree represents the possible moves of the opponent striving for minimum values. The final level of the tree contains the terminal nodes. Terminal nodes have no children nodes, and thus represent the final position of the game. The best final position for player would be integer 6, while the best final position for opponent would be 2.

FIG 7.20: *Recursion used to assign the minimum possible value to the left opponent node*

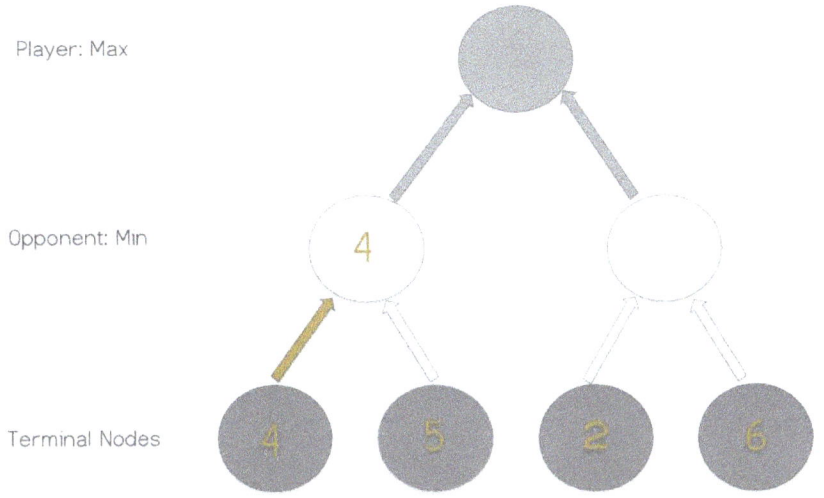

Here recursion is used to assign a value to a node based on what the children node values are and whether the current node wants the max or min value. The algorithm will begin at the root calling for children values. Since the root's children nodes are empty, the algorithm will travel down to level 1 of the tree to the left most node. At this node, it will once again call for the children nodes in which the values 4 and 5 are found. Since it is at the opponent level, the lower value is chosen, the value 4 is assigned to the node. Now the algorithm moves back up the tree to the root and calls for the values of the children nodes. This process is repeated down the right subtree.

FIG 7.21: *Recursion used to assign the value 2 to the right opponent node*

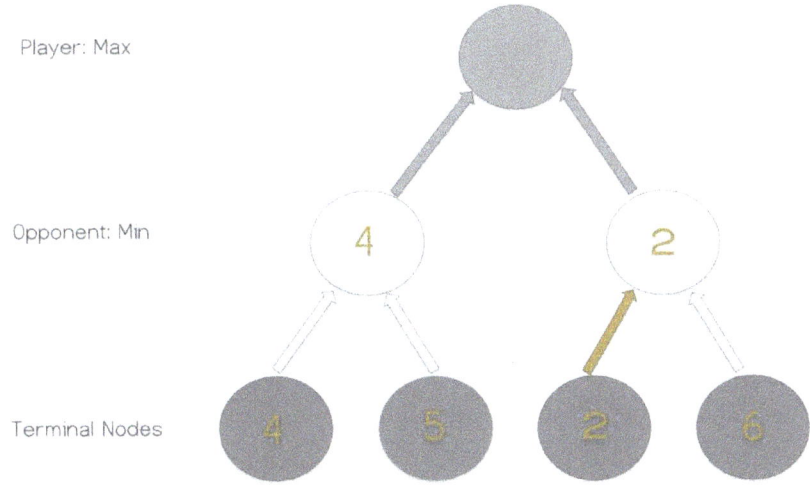

In the right subtree, the opponent is given the choice between 2 and 6. Once again, the algorithm assumes the minimum value and 2 is assigned to the parent node.

FIG 7.22: *The Root choses between the nodes of the opponent, higher value of 4 is assigned*

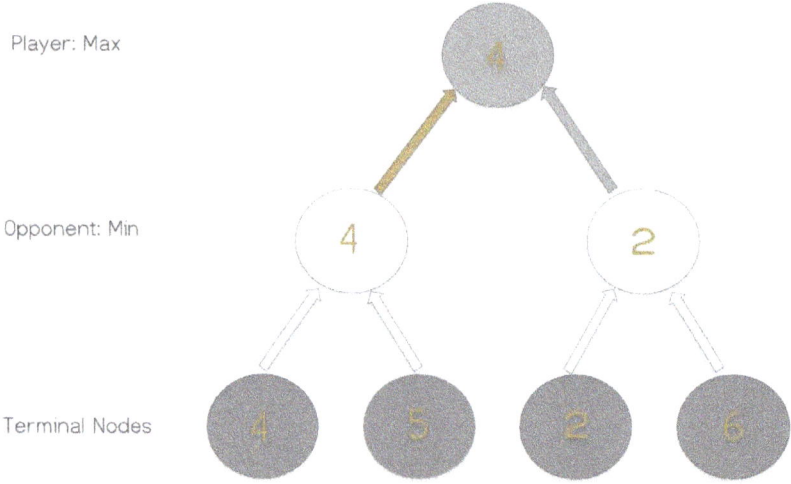

With the right subtree completed, the algorithm moves up once again to the root. Now, with the children nodes having assigned values, the player root is given an option between 4 and 2 based on the opponent's previous choices. Recall, the player wants to maximize the values. Easily, the player decides that 4 is indeed larger than 2 and the value 4 is assigned to the root.

FIG 7.23: *Final path of the player is decided*

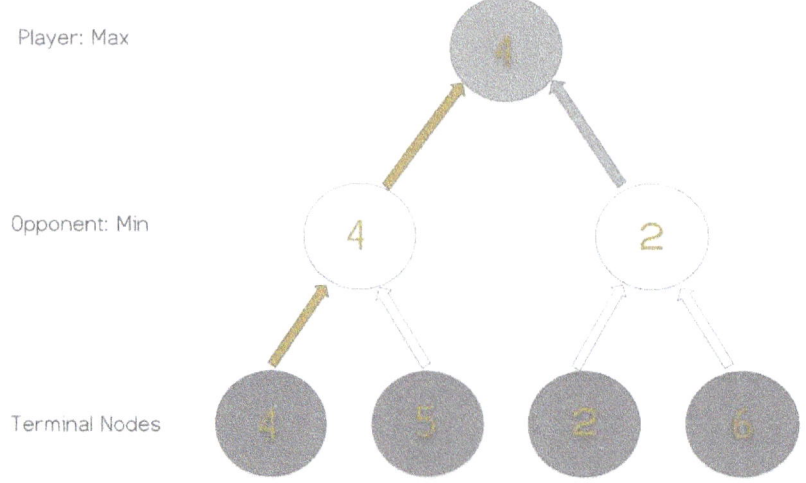

This path is the most optimal path for the player to choose given the opponent plays optimally as well. Value 6 would have been the best position for the player that exists on this game tree, but would never be able to achieve that position if the opponent played perfectly. Thus, 4 is the best value the player could achieve given the choices.

7.4 ALPHA BETA PRUNING

Since each node needs to be evaluated, the minimax algorithm is limited in its time complexity. In order to optimize this algorithm, **alpha-beta pruning** is used to reduce the computation time required. This technique is highly beneficial because it cuts or "prunes" off branches from the game tree that do not need to be searched since there is a better move available.

ALPHA AND BETA

The minimax algorithm stores a single value corresponding to the desirability of the node, either a max or a min value. In comparison, the minimax algorithm with alpha-beta pruning has two additional values: alpha and beta. Alpha is the best value for the maximizer along the path to the root, while beta is the best value for the minimizer along the path to the root. Each node must remember its alpha and beta values. Alpha can only update when it is on the level looking for a maximum, while beta can only update when it is on the level looking for a minimum.

KEEP IN MIND

1) Alpha can only update in a maximum node, and beta can only update in a minimum node.
2) The value V corresponding to the desirability of the node can only be returned to its parent.
3) Alpha and beta can only be passed down from its parent.
4) Condition to prune the node from the tree: alpha >= beta.

HOW IT WORKS

Let's take a look at the previous example using the alpha-beta technique this time. First, initialize alpha to negative infinity and beta to positive infinity to represent the worst possible scenario. A node can be pruned once alpha is greater than or equal to beta. Let's call the value corresponding to the desirability of the node to be value V. Value V is also initialized to negative infinity for a maximizer node and positive infinity for a minimizer node in order to represent the worst possible scenario.

FIG 7.24: *Alpha and beta values are assigned to the nodes with values of -∞ and ∞ respectively*

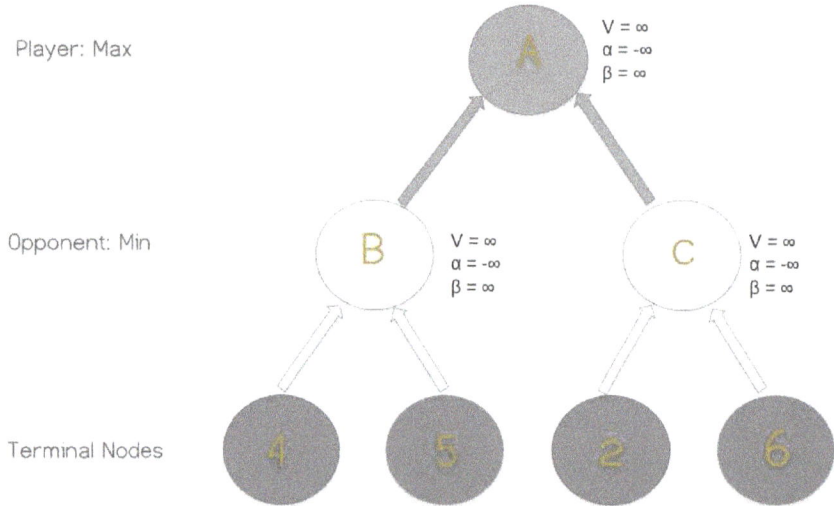

The initial call starts at the root of the tree, in this case node A. These alpha and beta values are passed down to the next child node, in this case node B. Node B will start by looking at its left child, which is a leaf node. The left child will return a value of 4. Value V of node B will now update to 4, since 4 is less than the current value V, positive infinity. Node B is a minimizer, so only the beta value will change. If the value V is less than the current beta value, the beta value will be updated. Since 4 is less than the current value of beta (infinity), beta is now equal to 4.

FIG 7.25: *The beta value for Node B is assigned 4*

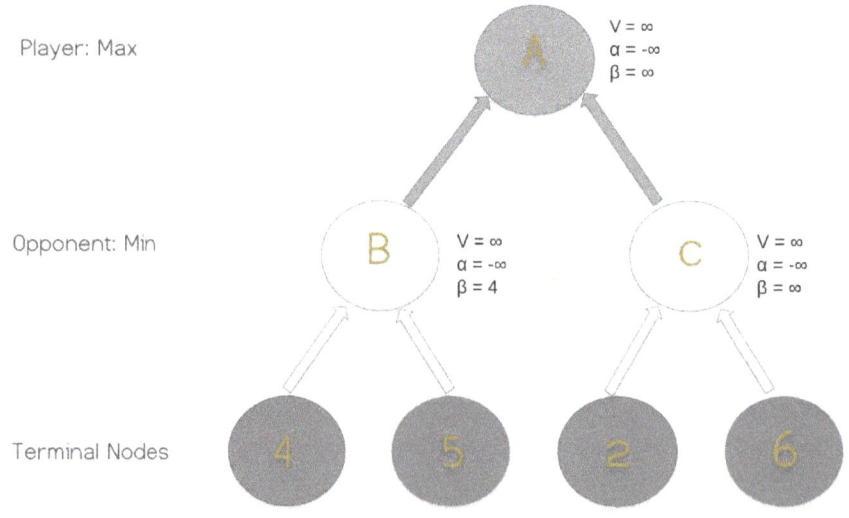

After comparing value V to beta, the algorithm will now compare alpha and beta to determine whether the tree can be pruned. If alpha is greater than equal to beta, the tree can be pruned so the second child does not need to be compared. In this case, alpha is less than beta because negative infinity is less than 4. Thus, the tree cannot be pruned and the second child must be compared to beta. The right child will return a value of 5. Since the current value V is less than 5, the value V will not change. Thus, beta will stay the same and the value of node B is 4.

FIG 7.26: After comparing with the right child, the value of Node B is now 4

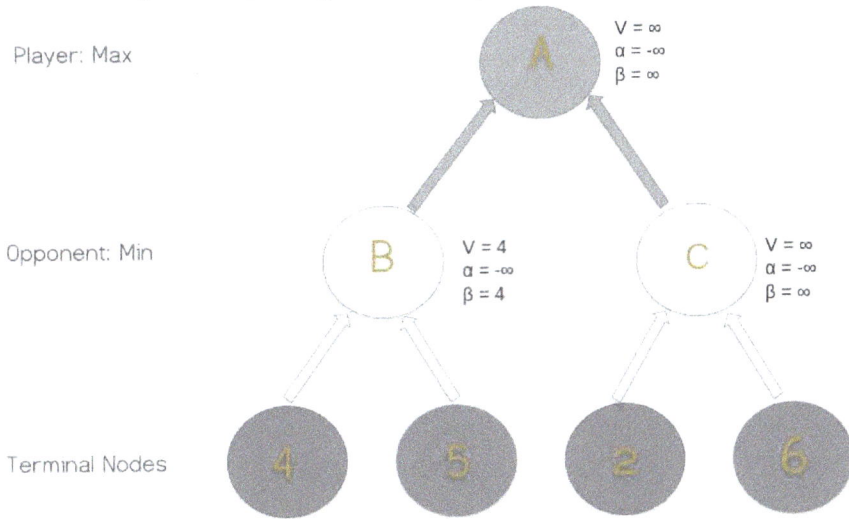

Next, the value V of node B is returned to its parent, node A. Value V of node A will now update to 4, since 4 is greater than the current value, negative infinity. Node A is a maximizer, so only the alpha value will change. If the value V is greater than the current alpha value, the alpha value will be updated. Since 4 is greater than the current value of alpha (negative infinity), alpha is now equal to 4.

FIG 7.27: *Value and alpha value is based to the parent node of B, node A*

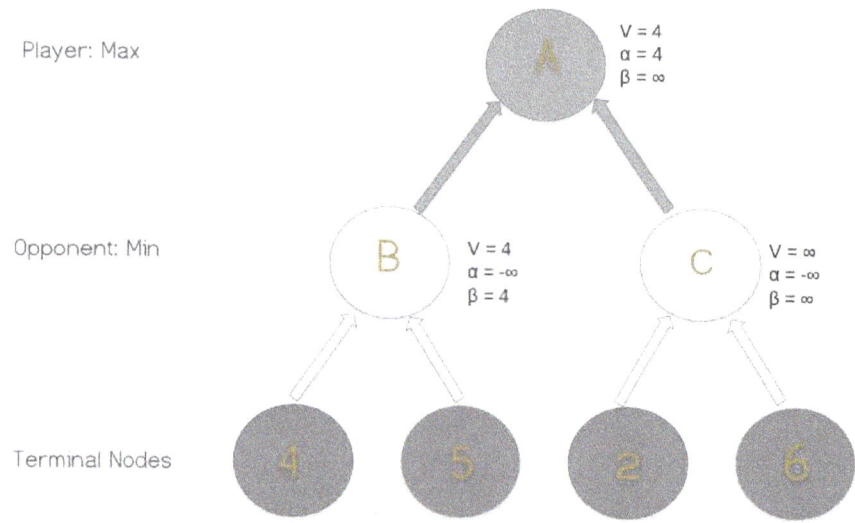

Since alpha is less than beta, we must continue checking the rest of the tree. These alpha and beta values are passed down to the next child node, in this case node C.

FIG 7.28: *Alpha value of 4 is passed from the node A to child node C*

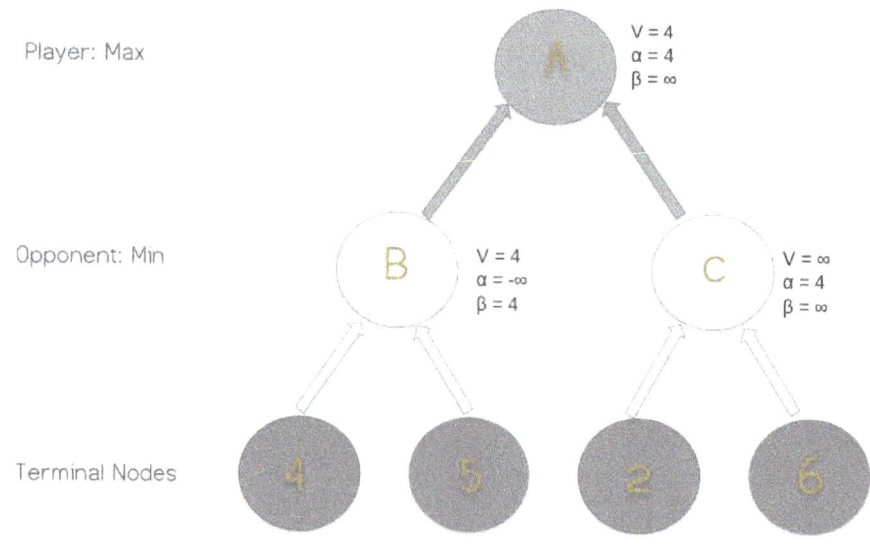

Once again, Node C will start by looking at its left child, which is a leaf node. The left child will return a value of 2. Value V of node C will now update to 2, since 2 is less than the current value V, positive infinity.

Node C is a minimizer, so only the beta value will change. If the value V is less than the current beta value, the beta value will be updated. Since 2 is less than the current value of beta (infinity), beta is now equal to 2.

FIG 7.29: Beta value of node C updates to 2 from the left child node

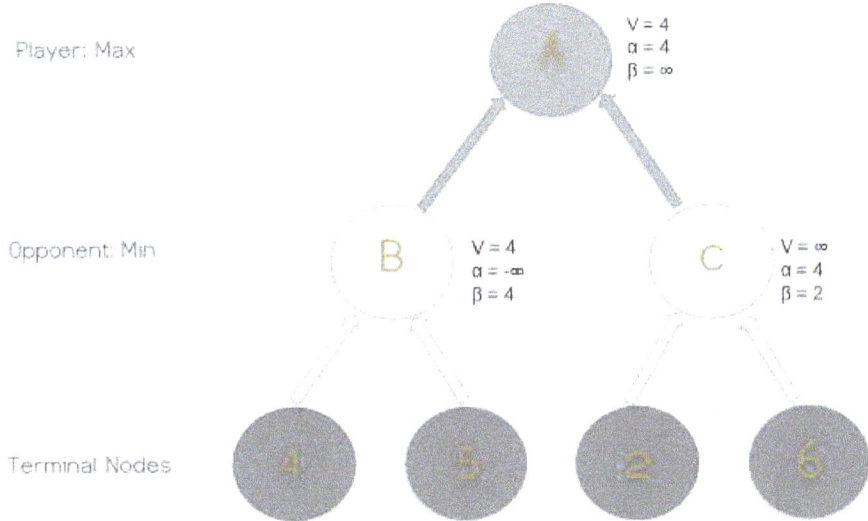

After comparing value V to beta, the algorithm will now compare alpha and beta to determine whether the tree can be pruned. If alpha is greater than equal to beta, the tree can be pruned so the second child does not need to be compared. In this case, alpha is greater than or beta because 4 is greater than 2. Thus, the tree can be "pruned". The logic works because since alpha is 4, anything less than 4 will not be considered by the node A above. After all, node A is a maximizer, meaning it is searching for the maximum value. Since one of the potential maximums is 4, the value sent up must be greater than 4 for it to matter, and node C will only send a value less than or equal to 2 because it is a minimizer. No matter what the value is at the right child of node C, it cannot be simultaneously less than 2 and greater than 4.

FIG 7.30: *Node C's right child is pruned as a better option is possible for player*

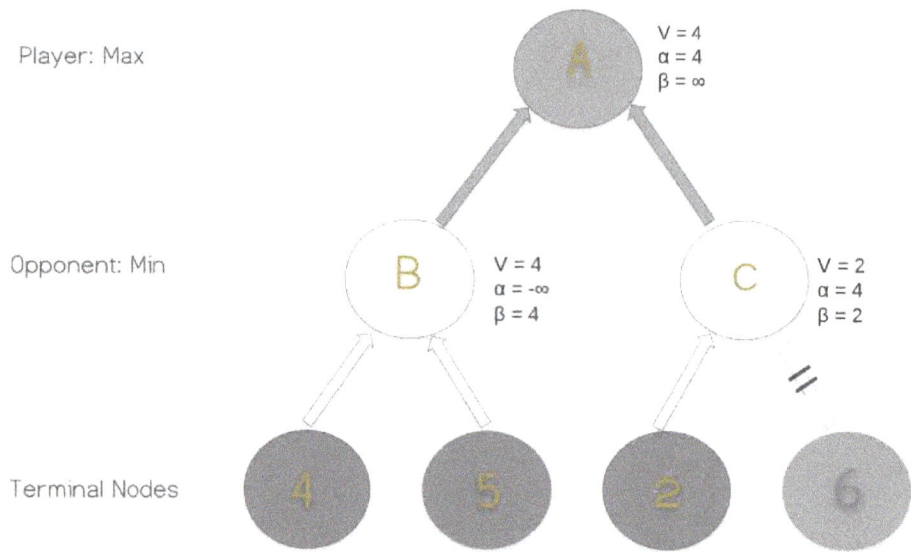

Next, the value V of node C is returned to its parent, node A. Value V of node A will not change, since the current value V of 4 is greater than 2. Thus, the optimal value for the maximizer node A is 4, so the best value the player can achieve is 4.

FIG 7.31: *Final Value of 4 is the best possible for player to achieve*

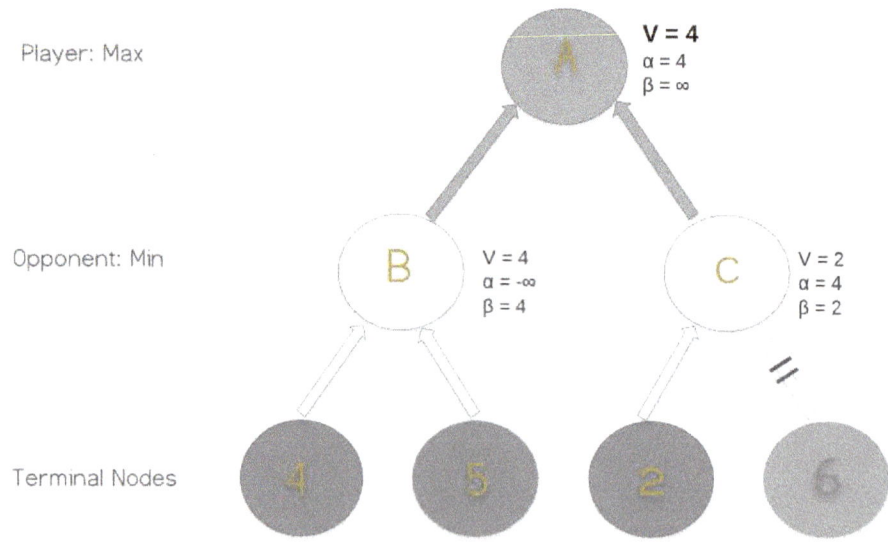

The minimax algorithm produces the same result with and without alpha-beta pruning. However, alpha-beta pruning can save a lot of computation time. With bigger game trees, alpha-beta pruning is much more efficient.

Appendix 1 Glossary

abstraction	allows one to think abstractly and utilize something without understanding how the small details work (**example**: driving a car without understanding the components of the brake system or engine); characteristic of object-oriented programming
arguments	input; values that are passed to constructors and methods
base case	smallest, most simple version of a problem (**example**: 0!, or 1, for factorials); once reached, a recursive method stops calling itself
Big O notation:	mathematical notation that refers to the time-complexity of an algorithm; explains how the runtime of an algorithm grows as the size of the input grows (**example**: O(n) signifies that the runtime will increase proportionally to the input size)
binary search	way of looking for a search key within a sorted search set in which half of the search set is eliminated at a time until the search key is found
binary tree	a tree in which each node has at most two child nodes
breadth first search	searching technique for a tree in which nodes of the same level are searched before moving to a higher level to find a key
bubble sort:	way of sorting data in which each element is compared to the adjacent element and the positions of the elements are swapped when necessary
bugs	errors in code
class	basic template for objects; can be thought of as a cookie-cutter
complete	binary tree in which every level has 2^l expect the final

binary tree	level
constructor	special function within a class that is automatically called when a new object is created; initializes field if necessary
data structure	organized collection of data
deadline	time by which a task must be completed
declaration	process of giving a variable a name and declaring its variable type
default constructor	constructor with no parameters that is automatically created when a class does not have an explicitly defined constructor; calls constructor of the superclass or assigns a null value to any unassigned variables if there is no superclass
depth first search	searching technique in which a key is matched with nodes of a tree first at the root then to the lower nodes of the tree before backtracking
Dijkstra's algorithm	well-known shortest path algorithm
doubly linked list	data structure with dynamic size in which elements are stored in nodes; each node holds data, a reference to the following node, and a reference to the previous node
duration	amount of time it takes for a task to complete
dynamic	able to change; when referring to the size of a data structure, it means that the size can be altered
dynamic memory allocation	memory is managed at runtime as the program executes

earliest deadline first	scheduling algorithm that executes tasks according to their deadlines so that the task with the earliest deadline executes first
edge	path between two vertices on a graph
encapsulation	data hiding; characteristic of object-oriented programming
else statement	conditional statement that follows an if statement; if the conditions of the if statement are not met, the code in the else statement will execute
extends	keyword for creating a subclass; subclass extends parent class
field	variable in a class that stores an attribute or value
fixed	unable to change; when referring to the size of a data structure; it means that the size can't be altered
First Come First Serve (FCFS)	scheduling algorithm that executes tasks according to their arrival times so that the task that arrived first executes first
heap	a data structure mapped as a complete binary tree
if statements	conditional statement; if the conditions of the if statement are met, the code in the if statement will execute; if the conditions are not met, the code in the else statement will execute
index	integer that indicates the position of an element in an array
inheritance	allows subclasses to inherit and use traits of parent classes; characteristic of object-oriented programming

in-place sorting algorithm	type of sorting algorithm that sorts a data structure "in-place; does not require extra memory to sort; the sorted structure occupies the same amount of memory the unsorted structure did
insertion sort	sorting process in which a single element of an array is compared to the element to the left of it and compared to see if they must switch until the entire array is sorted
instantiation	process of creating an instance (**example**: an object is an instance of a class, so we'd instantiate a class to create an object)
invoking	process of calling something to action
is-a	relationship between a subclass and its superclass; the subclass is-a superclass
linear search	way of looking for a search key within a search set that compared the search key to every element in the search set
linked list	data structure with dynamic size in which elements are stored in nodes; each node holds data and a reference to the following node
list	data structure with dynamic size which elements are stored in a contiguous fashion
matrix	two-dimensional array
merge sort	sorting technique in which an array is divided into sub arrays and merged together while being sorted
method	function

minimax algorithm	algorithm that finds the best case scenario for a player given that the opponent is playing perfectly
minimax algorithm with alpha-beta pruning	minimax algorithm that reduces the number of nodes that must be evaluated
modifiers	keywords that determine the accessibility of a class, constructor, method, etc.
node	object of class Node that holds non-primitive data and a reference to the next node in its linked list
null	empty
object	an instance of a particular class
object-oriented programming (OOP)	programming language with three specific characteristics: encapsulation, inheritance, and polymorphism
override	redefining a variable, constructor, or method
package	collection of modules
parameters	placeholders used to specify the type of information that methods and constructors need to execute
polymorphism	allow methods to be overridden at runtime; characteristic of object-oriented programming
primitive data type	basic data type supported by a programming language; basic building block for other data types

priority	level of importance; in a priority queue, elements are ordered according to their priority
priority queue	data structure in which elements are ordered according to their priority; the element with the highest priority is the first to leave the priority queue
private	modifier used to restrict access to a class, constructor, method etc.
public	modifier used to allow access to class, constructor, method, etc.
queue	data structure with a "first in, first out" policy
quick sort	in-place sorting algorithm that uses partitioning to sort data; recursive
recursion	process of calling a method by itself to simplify a problem down to its base case
reference	value that stores the location where a certain piece of data resides in memory
root vertex	first vertex in a shortest path sequence
runtime	when a program is being executed
search key	value being searched for
selection sort	sorting process in which each round the smallest algorithm is placed at the end of a sorted sub array
stack	data structure with a "last in, first out" policy
subclass	child class of a superclass

time-complexity	the amount of time taken by an algorithm with respect to the input size; quantification o the efficiency of an algorithm
traverse	visiting elements sequentially within a data structure
variable	reference to a memory location storing a specific value
vertex	point on a graph
virtual	keyword used to override methods
weight	cost of traveling an edge

Appendix 2: Acknowledgements

This is the third edition of the book, *Data Structures and Advanced Algorithms*. The first edition was written in Java by Shivana Anand, Emily Beck, Hang Cao, Joshua Culmer, and Emma Wood. Written in Python, this edition expands upon the material with the addition of more sorting techniques, searching techniques, and data structures. Similar to the first edition, this book was written in conjunction of a Boeing internship. No Boeing resources were used in the creation of this book.

www.ingramcontent.com/pod-product-compliance
Lightning Source LLC
Chambersburg PA
CBHW040539220526
45473CB00016B/2980